Oh, By the Way, I Have a Mental Illness

I Hate Being Bipolar, but It Has Actually Helped Me Have a Great and Fulfilling Life

by Michael Trzcinski

Title: Oh, By the Way, I Have a Mental Illness
I Hate Being Bipolar, but It Has Actually Helped Me Have a Great and Fulfilling Life

Copyright© 2018, all rights reserved
Published by Trzcinski & Company LLC
2567 Fenwick Rd.
Cleveland, Ohio
www.trzcinski.com

ISBN: 978-692-92062-6

TABLE OF CONTENTS

CHAPTER 1

My Name Is Mike

I'm a regular guy from Cleveland. I'm a good man — an honest and capable husband, son, employee and musician.

I'm creative and adventurous.

I've got a ton of empathy.

I love my life.

Oh, by the way, I've got a mental illness. It's not the main thing about me but it's important.

I'm bipolar. If I were to suddenly stop my medications, I would cycle radically from "up" to "down" and back again.

I have no intention of stopping my meds. I'm in great shape today. My mood swings are much less severe than they were in the past. But I've had some terrible times over the course of my life. Some years ago, when I was 39, I developed a plan to kill myself and spent time in a psychiatric hospital. I screamed "F--- you God!"

This book will examine my struggle with this disorder: how it went undiagnosed for years, how it got to the point where I cursed God, and how I finally got some help. I hope I can help some folks by describing the mistakes I made.

I also want to describe some positive things I've accomplished in my life. I believe my illness has contributed significantly to my ability to be creative, connect emotionally with people, and give service. I wouldn't trade my adventures and accomplishments for anything.

I raised money for, and helped build, a school in Indonesia where hundreds of bright-eyed kids of several faiths have been educated. I can stand in front of that school and say, "This is

something that actually makes a difference in the world!"
I've held several interesting jobs. I've evaluated hundreds of advanced technologies and helped commercialize several dozen of them. (Don't worry, I won't mention them all in this book, just two or three.)

I worked as an operative for a U.S. national security organization doing undercover work overseas.

I worked for NASA, where my boss said, "Mike, I like the way you think. You think differently from everyone else here."

I have mastered the trumpet and written more than 30 compositions and songs.

I've learned several life lessons that I think are worth sharing. At the very least, I want to help you see that people with mental illnesses are capable and regular human beings.

(Oh — I pronounce my name "tra-ZIN-skee.")

*

I'll have plenty to say in this book about the complexities of bipolar illness. Here is basic background:

- It goes by several names: bipolar illness, bipolar disorder, bipolar spectrum disorder, and bipolar affective disorder. Years ago it was called manic depression.

- As I indicated earlier, we bipolar people are prone to swinging back and forth between two poles: on the one hand, *hypermania* (having tons of energy and feeling euphoric; you basically feel you can walk on water) and, on the other hand, *depression*. Both of these extremes cause distorted thinking, feelings and behavior.

- I have bipolar Type I disorder, which is more severe than Type II. In Type I, the elevations of mood are bigger and broader.

- Bipolar disorder results from an imbalance in brain chemistry. It affects, possibly, about nine million people in the U.S. (perhaps 2 to 3 percent of the adult population). For a lot of bipolar folks, it hasn't been properly diagnosed; many of these people self-medicate with alcohol and drugs.

- It can't be cured. It's a lifetime condition. But it can be effectively treated.

- The illness is often associated with increased creativity. Cool, huh? Unfortunately it's also associated with an increased risk of suicide and self-harm.

*

I also struggle with a condition called codependency. This is a complicated disorder that affects people in different ways. For me, it's worrying too much about other people, and having a deep-down, hard-to-shake feeling that everybody else's needs and feelings are more important than mine. I needed years of therapy to realize a simple fact: I have the right to say "No!" (I say it frequently now. Sometimes I say it in different languages: *"Nein!" "Nyet!"* Feels good!)

Bipolar disorder and codependency are central aspects of my life and provide a foundation for this book. I want to show in these pages that these conditions can affect anybody, even a regular guy from Cleveland. I want you to realize that when a TV show like "Law and Order" shows a bipolar person who's doing something bad, it's not typical of who we are, it's just some writer in Hollywood reaching for "motivation" for a script that's due tomorrow at 9 a.m. Most bipolar folks function very well *if treated properly.* We often demonstrate quite remarkable creativity, empathy and problem-solving talent.

*

Here are a few famous people from the past who may have had bipolar disorder: Beethoven, Michelangelo, Florence Nightingale, Mark Twain, Virginia Woolf and Emily Dickinson. (The website WholePsychiatry.com has a long list of such folks.) I should say that we can't know with absolute certainty about the psychological conditions of anyone from history who wasn't closely examined by a professional, but we can make educated guesses. A fair number of scholars have examined letters, diaries and other evidence from the past for hints about possible mental illnesses.

Winston Churchill, possibly the greatest statesman of the 20th century, may have been bipolar. Here's a link to an interesting article[1] about this aspect of the great man.

In recent decades, lots of famous folks have mentioned their struggle with bipolar disorder, including Dick Cavett, Jane Pauley, Richard Dreyfuss, Burgess Meredith, Mariette Hartley and Catherine Zeta-Jones. Patty Duke was one of the first celebrities to go public with her bipolar disorder; she wrote two good memoirs: *Call Me Anna* (1987) and *A Brilliant Madness* (1992).

Many writers have published memoirs that mention or examine their bipolar disorder, including Haroon Moghul, whose book *How to Be a Muslim: An American Story* came out in 2017.

A number of top athletes have talked publicly about their bipolar disorder, including the Olympic handball star Amy Gamble, the Australian rugby league footballer Tim Smith, the golfers Bert Yancey and Muffin Spencer-Devlin, and the NFL player Alonzo Spellman. The movie *Fear Strikes Out* (1957) is about the struggle of baseball player Jimmy Piersall with bipolar illness. The wonderfully inspirational film *The Flying Scotsman*

(2006) is about the bipolar struggles of Scottish racing cyclist Graeme Obree. The 1994 film *Cobb*, starring Tommy Lee Jones as the great Ty Cobb, is called by one online reviewer "one of THE MOST insightful movies into bipolar mania ever made!"

The writer and performer Stephen Fry is bipolar. His film *Stephen Fry: The Secret Life of the Manic Depressive* came out in 2006 and won an International Emmy.

The actor and athlete Jean-Claude Van Damme is bipolar. He offers a memorable comment: "I'm an extreme bipolar. ... When I was young, I was suffering those swing moods. In the morning, the sky was blue when I was going to school, and to me, the sky was black. I was so sad." Van Damme got on medications and has enjoyed a wonderful career.

I heard a few years ago that Vincent van Gogh was likely bipolar. I've always been very interested in van Gogh — I love his work — so I sought out Dr. Joseph Calabrese, a Cleveland psychiatrist, who presented a paper[2] about the artist. I asked him, "Do we really know that van Gogh was bipolar?" He said, "The evidence is very strong based on the 650 letters he wrote. I examined every letter and wrote my paper based on my reading and analysis."

If you want to get a feeling for the strangeness of bipolar disorder — the glory of it, the intensity, and the flat-out terror — take a look at van Gogh's painting "The Starry Night" while listening to Don McLean perform his classic song "Vincent (Starry Starry Night)." The combination is available on YouTube[3]. The 1956 film *Lust for Life* starring Kirk Douglas as van Gogh is an amazing examination of bipolar genius.

Despite all the famous historical figures who might have been bipolar, despite all the celebrities coming out of the closet with regard to bipolar disorder, our society still generates a ton of stigma and prejudice about this condition. This stigma shows up in TV shows that need a handy villain. It shows up in job discrimination and hurtful remarks. The stigma translates to shame, embarrassment, hiding, lack of proper diagnosis, and self-medication. It translates to people not seeking the best possible help, not being honest with their kids, and not applying for jobs for which they're qualified (or being turned down for jobs by unenlightened managers).

One of my goals with this book is to call out societal stigma for what it is: silly and destructive.

*

At age 64 I'm doing well. I've achieved balance. I have lots of energy and I love getting things done.

I believe that mental illness has helped my creativity and empathy.

Creativity

- drives my quest for diverse activities, for risk, for stimulating adventures and challenges.

- has helped me develop a deep appreciation for, and a profound love of, all forms of art including music. I love writing music.

Empathy

- has helped me make deep connections with people.

- has helped me commit to having good relationships with my family, friends and co-workers.

- has given me skills to enrich people's lives through my humanitarian projects in Borneo and my present-day volunteering.

Could I have been equally creative and empathetic minus the mental illness? Maybe. There are plenty of creative and empathetic people around who aren't mentally ill. What I know for sure is, my bipolar disorder has strongly enhanced my capacities in those two areas. This is true for a fair number of bipolar folks.

*

If I were to sum up my approach to life in 20 words or less, I'd say this: I don't focus on happiness; I focus on peace of mind. Happiness tends to follow.

One way I pursue peace of mind is by learning to accept life as it is. It's not useful for me to get angry about stuff that I have no control over; in fact, it's the opposite of useful. I'll have more to say about anger in the course of this book.

Another way I seek peace of mind is by having a balanced lifestyle. I balance hard work with plenty of time for relaxation, including backpacking and sailing. I exercise, eat well and volunteer. As I mentioned, I work at keeping healthy relationships with people.

I pray and meditate. In my opinion, these have been as important as my medical regimen in helping me manage bipolar disorder. I believe that prayer and meditation are not promoted nearly enough by many professionals who treat bipolar illness. (I discuss some of the latest research on meditation in the "Frequently Asked Questions" chapter at the end of this book.)

I also seek peace of mind by just sitting around doing nothing. We have a right to be lazy sometimes!

*

I hope to help people with this book. I'm a gold mine of experience and insight into bipolar disorder (not necessarily by choice!). As someone once said, "To know even one life has breathed easier because you have lived. This is to have succeeded."

CHAPTER 2

My Early Years

I had a normal, average boyhood.

This raises a key question: If I was so ordinary as a kid, how come I developed an illness that almost killed me? Well, one strong theory about bipolar disorder is that it's genetically *based* and environmentally *triggered*. Maybe it lay dormant in my genes during my early years and then somehow came forth at a later time.

I was born in 1953 in the Cleveland suburb of Garfield Heights. I was the second of six kids.

We were lower middle-class, I guess. My father constantly complained about money. His name is Joe Trzcinski; he's a trumpet player, a really good one, for many years a "first-call" player for musical work in Cleveland. He probably could have made a great living if he had settled in Los Angeles, New York or Las Vegas, where he could have been the first-call studio and/or performance guy. He could have been part of Tower of Power, the greatest of all horn bands, or the Wrecking Crew, the team of L.A. musicians used by Phil Spector on all those hit records like "Be My Baby." But, well, he didn't. My mother liked Cleveland so they stayed there.

My dad often played seven nights a week. He performed at dinner theaters, ice shows, circuses, a Cleveland-area summer theater known as Musicarnival. He was the musical contractor for Cleveland's Front Row Theater for 22 years. He toured as part of Liberace's orchestra and with the musical *A Chorus Line.* He played in the orchestra when well-known singers and ensembles came to town (the Four Tops, the Temptations, the

Metropolitan Opera). He played with a young Stevie Wonder at the legendary Leo's Casino. He was a popular teacher of the trumpet with as many as 30 students at a time, including me, starting when I was 8. I played trumpet professionally by my teens. My brother John became a professional pianist; my nephew Chris is a top drummer.

I admired my dad (and still do, of course). I thought he was cool. He was energetic, talkative, the life of the party. He would head out of the house at 6 p.m. for an 8 p.m. gig dressed in a tux, carrying his trumpet case, with the Frank Sinatra vibe—smooth, elegant, a slight hint of Zizanie cologne as he walked past.

Meanwhile, my mother, Pauline, held the family together. She was always there, always calm and focused.

Mom and I were close when I was growing up. We would watch *Saturday Night at the Movies* on NBC together. Before the movie started, Mom would give me a quarter and I'd hike down to Pigeon's, a convenience store, and buy a bag of barbecue potato chips. Back home, we would eat the chips, drink home-made lemonade, and watch the movie — just the two of us. I remember seeing *The Desert Fox: The Story of Rommel* starring James Mason and *Demetrius and the Gladiators* starring Victor Mature. I would say to her, "When I get older, I'm going to be rich. I'm going to have you and Dad over every Saturday night, and we're not going to eat potato chips, we're going to have lobster!" Lobster, to me, was the ultimate food. She replied, "That's very nice, Michael." (Years later, when I offered to buy them a lobster dinner, Mom said, "That's very nice, Michael. Instead of lobster, can we have Alaskan king crab legs?")

Mom was, and is, very religious. We were a devout Catholic family. I was an altar boy and attended St. Timothy's Catholic School.

One time, I complained about saying the rosary while kneeling on the hard floor. All of a sudden, a breeze came through the window, and the window frame knocked over a small statue of a saint. Whoa! One second I'm complaining, and the next second the statue is knocked over. You can imagine my mom — "That was a sign from God, Michael." (I think that's possible, actually.)

I had a lot of fun as a kid and felt free. One time in kindergarten, I ran away during recess with a pal of mine. He went right home; I walked around for a couple of hours checking out the neighborhood. Mom was upset but didn't punish me. She just said, "O.K., well, watch TV if you want." (Can you imagine, a 5-year-old boy wandering around alone on the streets for hours? The world was different in 1958.)

Every morning in the summertime I wolfed down a huge breakfast — a quart of orange juice, maybe a half-dozen pancakes, maybe bacon and eggs with four pieces of toast — and met up with my friends. We stayed outside until dark except for coming home to get food. We biked. We schmoozed. We ran around in "The Woods," 20 acres of undeveloped land full of trees and bushes, with a 10-foot-wide creek running through it, perfect for playing war, like Sgt. Saunders in *Combat!*, which debuted on ABC in 1962 when I was 9 years old. I don't know who legally owned The Woods in 1962 but the real owners were a bunch of kids ages 8 through 12.

On summer evenings we played kick-the-can, pom-pom bullrush (also known as bulldog), and of course hide-and-seek. ("Apple peaches pumpkin pie, who's not ready holler I." The guy who lived across the street always yelled "I!")

When I about 7 years old, I was running full speed when I tripped. I very nearly fell into an uncontrolled, head-first, five-foot spill onto solid concrete. I was saved when a friend of mine stuck out his hand, flipped me over and saved me.

(I've had several close calls with death or major injury in my life. One time while sailing, I narrowly avoided a huge, unexpected storm that sank several boats. Once while backpacking on a mountain trail, a long way from civilization,

I lost my balance and hit my head hard on a rock. I made it to safety and said a little prayer. Maybe someone upstairs is watching out for me.)

*

One night when I was about 12, my friends and I made hangman's nooses out of pieces of rope and threw them over the streetlights to create ersatz gallows. The scene looked cool but pretty creepy too. The next morning the police were on the scene asking a lot of questions. They had apparently been summoned by our black neighbors, who were probably thinking, "Oh my God, KKK." We totally did not intend anything like that; we were just horsing around. I felt pretty bad about it and still feel guilty for causing pain for my neighbors and friends.

I should mention a key fact about my neighborhood during those years. It changed from mostly white to mostly black. Real estate companies were "block busting," i.e., persuading white homeowners to sell their property cheaply, out of fear that black folks would move into the neighborhood. The agents would resell at a higher price and laugh all the way to the bank. Block busting was a nasty practice but it was common in those years in many cities.

*

As I say, I believe my upbringing was fairly normal. One of the themes of this book is, anyone can have a mental health challenge — even a regular guy from Cleveland. Even your neighbor. Even someone in your family who you think is doing fine.

Even you.

I believe that mental illness is underreported in this country. I find support for this conviction in a paper published in the journal *JAMA Psychiatry* in 2014, based on long-term research at Johns Hopkins University. The paper says "the prevalence of mental disorders may be substantially higher than previously thought."

May be substantially higher — a pointed and bleak phrase. Disorders may be undiagnosed (or misdiagnosed) in millions of people. These people are ashamed, or in denial, or don't have access to good care, or believe that God intends them to suffer, or believe that their need for two stiff vodka tonics every night is nothing to worry about. So they don't try to get help.

Some towns have no affordable mental health care. Maybe there's one free clinic in the whole town. Maybe it's on the other side of town; maybe a guy has to take three buses to get to it. (Maybe there are no buses.) Once he gets there, he waits an hour for an overworked, overstressed, inexperienced counselor who sees 25 people a day, works 12 hours a day and makes $35,000 a year.

In my opinion, we would benefit as a society by investing more taxpayer dollars in good mental health care, including better salaries for the dedicated therapists who work in the public health sector. Greater investment in this area would result in a healthier and more productive workforce, a stronger economy and, maybe, more happiness.

*

I asked my parents recently about our family history, about relatives who showed unusual behavior back in the day. I'm curious about genetic connections that may have generated my bipolar disorder.

My grandfather (my mother's father) went through 24 bottles of beer every weekend plus more when his brothers visited. Seems like a lot. I'm not sure how booze affected Grandpa but I doubt it did him much good.

My father's aunt, Aunt Elizabeth, might have had an undiagnosed bipolar disorder. Three incidents from her life suggest the manic phase of the illness: One of her children came home one day after being shortchanged on meat at the local butcher shop. Elizabeth ran down to the shop in a rage and smashed its glass display case, badly cutting her hand. Another time, she abruptly left her family of nine children and went to Massachusetts for a number of days — we don't know why. Still another time, she hid in the bushes waiting for her daughter to return from a date with a guy Elizabeth didn't like. When they arrived, she jumped out of the bushes and started beating the boyfriend with an umbrella.

*

I buried my feelings when I was a boy. I kept my mouth shut to keep the peace. I would acquiesce to others because I thought they were more important.

I squashed my anger down under layers of armor. I didn't know what anger was until I was in my 30s. Amazing, huh? Only after getting into therapy did I realize how much crap I had been blocking off internally.

I've learned there are ways to manage anger, to let it out, to let it go. I don't consider myself unduly angry today. I'll mention here a quote from Prevention magazine: "Learning how to express rage can protect your heart, mind, health."

What was I so angry about when I was a kid? I really don't know. Maybe it was genetic.

Did my buried anger somehow contribute to the development of my bipolar disorder? I don't know.

Did the buried anger contribute to the development of my codependency? Perhaps there are connections there.

Writing is helpful in coming to grips with anger. There's a wonderful book on this subject called *Expressive Writing:*

Words That Heal (2004) by James H. Pennebaker and John F. Evans. Also good: *The Anger Control Workbook* (2000) by Matthew McKay and Peter Rogers. A fine book aimed at kids is *How to Take the Grrr Out of Anger* (2015 revised edition) by Elizabeth Verdick and Marjorie Lisovskis.

*

The role of peacekeeper, caretaker, problem-solver came naturally to me in my family.

On Thanksgiving Day in 1965, when I was 12, my mom was in the hospital after giving birth to her sixth child, my little sister, Joanne. I cooked Thanksgiving dinner for the family. No one told me to do it; I wanted to do it.

I called my mom on the phone and got directions. She said, "Preheat the oven to 350. Make a little tent out of aluminum foil. Baste the turkey."

"What does 'baste' mean, Mom?"

"Spoon the juices over the turkey to keep it moist."

If I hadn't cooked that bird, we would have eaten Swanson's TV dinners while watching the football game, and my dad would have said, "This is the worst Thanksgiving ever." Our meal turned out great. I felt proud.

I worried about the family's money. When my mom was pregnant with Joanne in '65, I asked her, "How can we afford a baby?" That's a pretty heavy question for a 12-year-old to be asking.

I studied interest rates carefully. When I was 15, I got 5 percent interest for my account at a local savings and loan. My parents were getting 4 percent at a bank. Other places paid 4.5 percent, 4.8, etc. I translated various percentages into dollars, sat down at the kitchen table with Mom and Dad, showed them the figures ("O.K., $500 over two years at 5 percent becomes…") and convinced them to switch.

I always felt we were poor even though we weren't. The feeling of not having money bugged the heck out of me.

I resolved to be financially secure by the time I was 18 so that I could pay for college (my Dad told me that he and Mom wouldn't be able to help me there), get a good job and make a really good salary. I didn't want to be a financial burden to my parents; I didn't want to cause them the tiniest bit of trouble ever. (That, by the way, is an early sign of my codependency, i.e., I didn't merely worry about their feelings, I obsessed.) I wanted complete control of every aspect of my life. I hated others telling me what to do. For me, money equaled freedom.

I worked like crazy starting at a young age. When I was 12 I got a morning paper route, which I kept for years, rolling out of bed every day at 6 a.m. and getting *The Plain Dealer* onto people's porches. I'd go collecting once a month and accumulate a bunch of $1 bills. I would pin these to my T-shirt, 30 or 40 of them, and admire myself in the mirror for a minute or two. I would show my get-up to my mother, who would say something positive like, "Michael, you work hard for your money!" I'd remove the pins, put the bills in a nice stack, walk a mile to the bank, and put the money into my savings account. I loved my bankbook. I loved watching the numbers get higher and higher.

When I was 14 I got a job at McDonald's. Twice a week I walked two and a half miles to work as an order-taker for a couple of hours at $1 per hour. I got a discount on cheeseburgers and ate a lot of them. All these years later, I can't even look at those things without gagging.

When I was 16 I got a job at a retail store called Whale's Tale that sold nautical hardware in the summer and giftware in the winter. I became an expert on every product in the store: sail battens, rubber dinghies, engines.

Meanwhile, I played the trumpet professionally in several bands including a Motown group, various touring shows including *Man of La Mancha*, and for the singer Lou Rawls. I played in a concert band at high school, a jazz band, a marching band, and with Case Western Reserve University's concert band. And I practiced my instrument an hour a day.

One cool thing I did during this period was organize a 200-mile canoe trip for myself and two friends in Ohio. It was a GREAT trip! I loved getting out and doing stuff like that.

I went to school and studied to maintain a strong grade point average. As I aimed for college, I realized a couple of basic facts about life: (1) You have to work for everything; and (2) You're on your own. I wasn't going to get help from anyone else in achieving my goals.

I didn't think I needed any help. I had unbelievable drive and energy. I loved my life. I loved being busy; I noticed I was happiest when I was totally busy all day long. I remember saying in the summer of 1969, "I LOVE being 16! I never want to grow up!"

This was a "hypomanic" state, I eventually learned, also known as "mildly manic." It's the "up" side of bipolar.

Being mildly manic is a great state — you can get a lot done and stay in reasonably good control. I may have been mildly manic for a full year leading up to the autumn of '69.

I thought I was in a groove that would last forever. Then I crashed into depression.

*

One week I was full of zest; the next week I could barely move, and saw no escape from a gray abyss. That's bipolar disorder in a nutshell. (As I indicated earlier, the condition was still called manic depression in 1969.)

To the best of my recollection, this was my first encounter with the illness. But I didn't know it was an illness. I had no idea what was going on. I thought it was a normal part of growing up.

I never said anything to anyone about what was happening with me.

I would cry myself to sleep at night thinking about suicide. I obviously needed help but I didn't ask for it and didn't get any.

I was totally dispirited in September of '69 when I started my junior year of high school. One day when I walked into religion class, the teacher looked at me, frowned, and asked, "Michael, are you always this depressed?" I had no idea what he was talking about. I probably had never heard the word "depressed" before. I replied, "I guess?"

That teacher was a brother in the Marianist religious order (the Society of Mary). He presumably had some knowledge about helping people. As I think back now on this encounter, I wish he had asked more questions and helped me find some answers. Instead, he just let the subject drop, and so did I. The concept of "intervention" by a teacher was not a high-priority topic in those days.

My depression lasted all autumn. I'm pretty sure that the autumn connection is important. Psychiatrists will tell you their phones ring off the hook in the fall — as the days get darker, some people lose their mental and emotional balance. We humans carry a profound awareness of the seasonal battle between dark and light. The darkness bugs us on some deep level; hence our joy when we see holiday lights in the darkest days of December.

All that autumn, when my alarm clock rang in the morning, I gritted my teeth and got out of bed. I had to get up. I had stuff to do. I was working 25 hours a week outside of school. Keeping busy helped me survive.

The depression began to dissipate, slowly, so that by Christmas of '69 I was holding things together pretty well. I was very tense though. One of my teachers, Bob Van Bergan, told my father, "I wish I could put my arm around Mike and have him relax."

Using medication to treat bipolar disorder wasn't common in 1969. That said, I'm really angry that nothing, nothing whatsoever, was done for me. The Marianist brother asked just that one question, and Bob offered just the "I wish" comment. (I want to add, Bob was one of my favorite teachers ever.)

During that school year, guidance counselors met with students to discuss college and careers. One by one everyone was called ... except me. I really wanted to go because I thought I could get some help with the emotional issues I was facing. But I never got the call; to this day I don't know why. I was definitely college material; my grade point average was 3.67. I have a special place in my heart for teenagers who aren't getting the help they need.

I would like to interject a thought here. I think that when teens suffer from a severe illness such as bipolar disorder, they can experience arrested development. Self-esteem and basic interpersonal skills can stop maturing. I think this happened with me.

I should mention another factor in my struggle during these years. I developed severe acne at age 14. This did quite a number on my self-esteem. I never had a date in high school; I was too self-conscious to talk to girls.

I finished high school in June 1971. I had $5,600 in the bank. I started college that fall at Ohio State, and I paid for everything: tuition, room, board, books and incidentals, about $2,200 a year altogether. This was a major accomplishment in my life and it gave me a lot of satisfaction and confidence. (I continued working during my college years, summers and during the Christmas break.)

I graduated from Ohio State in 1975 with a degree in business. This, too, gave me major confidence. I was the first member of family to graduate from college. I stood there with my diploma, wearing the little mortarboard, and I thought, "I did it!"

I continued my education after college by traveling in Europe for four months, staying in youth hostels, keeping a journal, drinking it all in. What a great trip. Later on (1982) I earned a master's in business administration from Case Western Reserve. And from 1995 to 2000 I studied music theory and composition at the Cleveland Institute of Music.

*

During my first semester of college, a guy in my dorm said, "Hey Mike, you might be able to get some help for that acne. Tetracycline. It worked for me." He was referring to an antibiotic that was popular with dermatologists for acne in the early '70s and is still widely prescribed today for the condition. I went to the health service and got some. The acne cleared up in a week — this, after four years of hating my face. I thought, "Manna from heaven! I'm just like everyone else!"

Or so I thought.

CHAPTER 3

My Adventure In A Psychiatric Hospital

As I proceeded through high school and college, I had several periods of depression, but I never mentioned them to anyone. I didn't get my diagnosis of bipolar disorder until I was 25 years old, in 1978. Even then, I didn't adopt a consistent pattern of taking medications.

The result was a terrible crisis at age 39 when I planned to kill myself.

Here's the full story.

*

The doctor who gave me my diagnosis in 1978 was a neurosurgeon with expertise in psychiatry. Let's call him Dr. Weinstock. I discussed my thoughts of death with him, took some tests, answered some questions, and got the diagnosis: bipolar (it was still known as manic depression in those days).

Weinstock prescribed lithium carbonate for me, which I took for three weeks and hated. Hated!!! I felt that the drug robbed me of much of my personality, the fun and exciting parts, the highs. I experienced thick brain fog and slept very poorly. There are not enough swear words in the English language to express my hatred of lithium.

*

My opinion about lithium is fairly common in the bipolar community. Bipolar people often stop taking it, primarily because they miss their highs.

There are several kinds of lithium: aspartate, carbonate, chloride, citrate, orotate. Three of these are used for major depression and bipolar disorder: carbonate, citrate, and orotate. According to what I've read, lithium carbonate is the best form of lithium for 60 percent of bipolar people — i.e., it's great for more than half of us but not so great for many of us. It can have side effects beyond brain fog and insomnia, including diabetes insipidus and problems with the thyroid and liver.

(A historical note: The pioneer in using lithium to treat bipolar disorder was the Australian psychiatrist John Cade. A key American in this realm is Dr. Ronald R. Fieve; his important book *Moodswing* (1975) has sold hundreds of thousands of copies and has dramatically increased public awareness of bipolar Type II.)

*

Lithium helped me in some ways. It lifted me out of the deepest part of the depression trough and kept me from getting too high. I felt encouraged by this. I figured, well, heck, since it's helped me, I can stop taking the damn stuff! (I admit that was a weird thought.)

I proceeded to do just that. I avoided the meds and stopped seeing Dr. Weinstock. I stayed relatively stable. I was convinced I was all better. I didn't realize, or didn't accept, that bipolar disorder comes in cycles (the cycle times vary widely, from weeks to years).

In the middle of 1979, six months later after quitting the drug, I visited Dr. Weinstock again, told him I hadn't been depressed for all those months, and proudly announced, "See, I'm not bipolar!" He said, "I think you are, Mike."

I laughed him off.

I didn't accept the fact that I was sick. I didn't trust

27

the medical profession. I'm not sure why I was in such denial. Maybe it was because illness represented loss of control.

Several years passed. During this period I re-thought my position on lithium and arrived at a compromise stance I could live with. I said to myself, "*Maybe* lithium *might* do me some good if I figure out, on my own, how much to take and how often." I went to see a new doctor — we can call him Dr. Forrester — and informed him of my brilliant plan. He shrugged, said "OK," and prescribed me lithium. I took it for six or eight weeks. I still hated the stuff, but I felt better with it, and as soon I felt better, I stopped taking it.

I would see Forrester whenever I had a major manic or depressive episode, take the drug for a while, then stop. This pattern continued for years.

So we're up to 1987. This was the year I started praying at a monastery. I loved this. It helped me a lot.

I started praying because I was in a bad place at my job, worrying about being fired because I wasn't getting along with top management. I was feeling huge anxiety. I decided to pray every weekday morning at the Carmelite monastery (Carmel of the Holy Family) a couple of miles from our home in Cleveland. I benefited tremendously from going there every morning at 6:30 and spending an hour in silent prayer. (My wife, Luanne, came with me on Sundays.) I would walk into the beautiful little chapel, sit or kneel, and just ... pray. I prayed for peace of mind and self-acceptance. I prayed for world justice and peace.

My prayer eventually shifted to meditation. This, too, was great: I felt relaxed most of the day.

I regarded prayer and meditation as life-giving supplements, 100 percent natural and healthy. I felt deeply relaxed and centered, and what's more, I felt connected to all of life, past, present and future. I believed that God had led me to prayer and meditation and was saying, "Mike, use these tools to get better." I put myself in God's hands.

I swore off medicines and doctors. I figured that if I got into trouble, well, so be it. That's how God wants it. But I didn't expect problems. I expected to recover.

I stayed on this path for three years, but then, in 1990, everything fell apart.

I went into a deep depression. The effects of meditation (and they were excellent) apparently weren't enough to counteract the absence of medication.

I became incredibly angry because I had thought I had found a solution in prayer and meditation. I had thought God had given me the answer, and now he was snatching it away.

I had something to say to God:

"JUST LEAVE ME ALONE!"

I stopped meditating. I stopped visiting the monastery. I kept up with church on Sunday, accompanying my wife to services, but mostly I told God to quit messing with my life.

I was angry and felt every bit of my anger.

Then I had a thought:

"Maybe God is trying to tell me to *stay on my medications.*"

Verrrrry interesting!

I believe God sends messages to human beings but gives us the option of deciding whether to follow through. I'm thinking of a little story. A flood is coming. A woman is in her house. A bus comes by, sent by the Police Department, and the officers say, "We're taking people to a safe place." She says, "I'm going to stay here, God's going to save me."

The flood comes, there's three feet of water in her house. A boat comes by and the officers say, "We're taking people to a safe place." She says, "I'm going to stay here, God's going to save me." The water continues to rise; now she's on the roof. A helicopter comes by and the officers say, "We're taking people to a safe place." She replies. "I'm going to stay here, God's going to save me." The water continues to rise; a storm whips up; she drowns.

She arrives in heaven. She asks God, "Why didn't you save me?" God replies, "Hey, I did my best. I sent you the bus, the boat and the helicopter, but you ignored my messages."

*

To summarize my situation from my mid-20s to my late 30s, I didn't have a consistent pattern of taking medications. I only took the drugs sporadically — "by exception" is the term I used. My illness got worse over time because of the way I was handling it. My bipolar episodes became more frequent and extreme. The highs were very buzzy and supercharged, and the lows were the pits.

By 1990 and '91 my depressive lows were impossibly bad. Meanwhile, my second psychiatrist, Dr. Forrester, had lost his license for mis-prescribing medications. As it turns out, finding the right psychiatrist can involve a lot of trial and error, just like finding the right combination of drugs.

I started seeing a new psychiatrist in '91, a Dr. van Zandt. I said, "I'll do anything to get rid of this pain." She said, "The first things I want to start you on are regular lithium and Zoloft." I thought, "Oh, no, not lithium!" but I took it.

I got better in one way: I wasn't as depressed, the lows in the cycle weren't as low. But, as before, I felt as if part of my personality was taken away: my hypomania (my hopped-up cycle, where I had a lot of fun).

I felt the loss of the highs deeply. It actually put me in a state of mourning, much like a person would grieve the loss of an arm or leg.

What happened next, in the summer of '92, was disastrous.

Because I hated lithium so much and complained about it all the time, Dr. van Zandt finally said, "O.K., we'll try something else." Experimenting with different medications is common in mental illness and is part of the therapeutic process. Finding the best package is often trial-and-error. Dr. van Zandt's decision to try something else was entirely ethical and was consistent with solid medical thinking (she's a wonderful psychiatrist).

In September 1992, I went on a new drug, Tegretol (carbamazepine) as a replacement for lithium. This didn't work at all. I became full-blown manic, with incredible highs followed by terrible lows (in most cases you can't have one without the other if you're bipolar). Dr. van Zandt quickly spotted my mania and switched me back to lithium, but it was too late. The lows took over. I couldn't pull myself out. I was in so damn much pain.

*

I experience depression in several ways.

The worst is what I call severe painful clinical depression. I haven't experienced this for 25 years, but when I was young, it sometimes lasted for weeks or months.

During these sieges, I felt severe mental pain. I find it hard to describe this pain. My basic symptoms were fatigue, hopelessness and difficulty making decisions. I felt like the most worthless person in the world. I had recurring thoughts of suicide. I thought, "If I'm dead, then all the pain will stop." I found it hard to be engaged in activities, even things I usually liked to do, like going for a walk or watching a movie. I had to push myself to do anything at all. The one thing I did enjoy during those times was sitting at the piano and playing or writing a melancholy song.

The second type of depression, which I occasionally experience now, is what I call mild depression. It's similar in some ways to severe painful clinical depression but the symptoms are much milder. I don't get thoughts of harming myself. And it might last for only a day or a few days. It tends to be triggered by stressful events in my life. Meditation really helps me deal with this form of depression.

Then there is what I call a "flat state." I'm neither happy nor depressed. I'm just sort of quiet and non-engaged.

The other side of the bipolar scale is what's called "mania." I sometimes get into what's called slight, or hypomania. This is where I'm motivated, engaged, happy, dynamic, talkative. This mood might last for a few days.

*

Every day in the U.S., about 100 people kill themselves. Severe painful depression is a leading factor in many of these deaths. Since you started reading this chapter, somebody in this country probably committed suicide or tried to. The poor soul just wanted to get out of his or her pain. Perhaps their medications were not working, or they stopped taking them, or they never had the right meds to begin with.

I intended to kill myself in the autumn of '92 and had a plan for doing so.

*

One Friday morning in November of '92 I walked into Dr. van Zandt's office and plunked three bottles of drugs on her desk: lithium and Zoloft for depression and trazodone to help me sleep. I said, calmly, "These aren't doing me a bit of good. I'm giving you one week to get me un-depressed."

I was telling her, in a guarded way, that in one week I was going to kill myself if I still felt awful. She saw exactly what I was saying. She knew that suicidal thinking often progresses along a path and that I had almost reached the end of the path. When a suicidal person puts a definite time frame into the equation ("one week" or whatever it is), and has the means to do the job, it's a critical situation.

I didn't explicitly say, "I'm going to kill myself." No way. I was too canny for that. If I had uttered those words out loud, Dr. van Zandt and Luanne might have had me involuntarily committed.

The doctor and I spoke for an hour. She recommended that I increase my dosage of lithium and Zoloft and said I should strongly consider hospitalization. She asked me to come see her again on Monday.

As I drove home, I reviewed my suicide plan. I was going to drive to Florida, rent a catamaran, sail out into the ocean, put on heavy weights, shoot myself, and fall in the water. This method, I thought, would cause the least amount of grief for people and leave no mess to clean up. I would disappear into the deep with a big hole in my head and a lot of blood to attract sharks. Brilliant, right? I'm always thinking about others.

On Saturday morning I had a lot of trouble getting out of bed. During the day I was sad, confused, depressed — I didn't know what to decide about hospitalization. My brain was trying to navigate through a fog and wasn't making it.

On Sunday I sat alone in my living room and suddenly said out loud, "I'm out of control. I'm not perceiving reality correctly. I give up trying to do everything on my own. I give up, God!"

This was my rock bottom.

*

I went to see Dr. van Zandt on Monday and said, "I think I need to go in the hospital." As I spoke to her, I broke down crying.

She said, "I think the hospital is a good idea."

All my adult life I had said, "I will never check myself into a mental hospital no matter what. Never!" I've always had a fear of being locked up, whether in a prison or a hospital. The movie *Midnight Express* freaked me out — that poor guy getting locked up in a foreign country, my God, I could barely watch it. Same deal with *One Flew Over the Cuckoo's Nest*. I'm haunted by Jack Nicholson's fate in that film.

To me, a hospital meant giving up control. I had built my whole life around self-sufficiency.

On the other hand, I was desperate. I was 39 years old

and was not sure if I would see 40.

Luanne drove me to Windsor Laurelwood Hospital in suburban Cleveland on Monday, November 16, 1992. She hadn't realized how serious my depression was. We were sad to say goodbye to each other, but she was happy that I would be in a safe place getting good professional care.

*

I was met by a staff person named Elliott. He seemed to be a regular nice fellow — he wasn't wearing a white coat or anything like that, just an ordinary polo shirt and slacks. He smiled and said, "Hello Mike, welcome," and escorted me down a hallway.

I carried a small suitcase packed with clothes, a shaving kit and a few other essentials. We walked through two sets of locked doors controlled by a guard with a buzzer. Suddenly I got worried. I thought, "I might not get out!"

I had been OK with going into the hospital but I had not made a decision to get myself locked up — I didn't realize that locked doors and buzzers were part of the deal. I probably should have checked that out beforehand, but I didn't, and with the sound of the buzzers ringing in my ears, I had to stop for a minute and take a few deep breaths.

I knew I could walk out if I wanted to (I was voluntarily committed), but if I did so I would forfeit my insurance. In order for insurance to pay, you have to be officially discharged. I thought of the line from "Hotel California": "You can check out anytime you like, but you can never leave."

I swallowed my semi-panic. I thought about the importance of trust. I remembered to breathe. And I proceeded down the hallway.

I will say that my first impression of the facility was favorable except for the locked doors. Elliott was friendly. The physical surroundings were clean, quiet and comfortable — wide hallways, gentle lighting. It was like a Hampton Inn hotel — nice, in a functional way. Nobody screaming or anything like that.

It was early evening. People were in their rooms. Elliott and I walked past a number of rooms with doors shut, or halfway shut, and came to my room.

My roomate, a man named Frederick, was asleep when I came in. He was asleep most of the time I was there. He slept 20 hours a day, said Elliott, and hardly ever ate. He apparently checked himself into the hospital every few months to get away from regular life and sleep to his heart's content. Maybe he had a lot of stress in his life; maybe he had a Cadillac insurance plan or a ton of money. I think we spoke twice, briefly, during the three weeks of my stay: "Hi, Frederick." "Hi, Michael. Good night."

Elliott asked for my razor, belt and hair dryer, and took them away as a precaution. The belt and the hair dryer cord, he said, "could be used as a noose." (Noose — what a strange and terrible word. I flashed on the nooses I had flung over the streetlights in my neighborhood when I was a kid.)

He reached in his pocket and pulled out pulled a green wristband.

"Mike, I want to put this on you now."

"OK"

The wristband, said Elliott, was a signal to the staff that I was on suicide watch. Every 15 minutes, day and night, an attendant had to see me alive, in one piece, not bloody, not dead. Also, my movements were limited: I couldn't go to the cafeteria/dining room; my food would be brought to me.

Suicide watch. I pondered this phrase. I understood the need for it but I was taken aback by hearing it spoken aloud. Elliott said it gently, casually, but I felt like he was shouting at me, like I was 7 years old, in the second grade in a Catholic school, and he was roaring at me that I was bad and unworthy and doomed to burn for eternity.

Elliott shook my hand and departed. I sat on the bed for a few minutes. I looked down at the floor. I thought about the long, strange trip that that brought me to this place. I remembered how, when I was a kid, I cried myself to sleep.

I didn't cry now. I got down on my knees and asked God for assistance in the coming days.

*

I spent the next day resting and relaxing. I poked my head into the hallway a few times but mostly I stayed in my room, napped, wrote in my journal, and stared through a small window at a vacant lot and trees. There was no TV in the room. Frederick didn't snore, thank God.

The following day I was asked by one of my counselors to take a personality and health inventory, which involved hundreds of multiple-choice questions. I needed a full three hours to work through it. It was interesting stuff: "If a fire broke out in your home, what would you do first?" (Get out? Call 911? Try to put the fire out yourself? Notify other people in the house?) "What kind of film would you rather watch?" (A movie about a romantic relationship? An action movie about World War II? A documentary about an interesting travel destination? A horror movie where lots of people get killed?)

On the third day I had a major breakthrough: I was taken off suicide watch. They gave me a white wristband to replace the green one. I gazed at my new wristband and thought, "Well, progress is being made!" With the new wristband I could walk to the cafeteria for meals. Yeah baby! This was highly symbolic to me.

At the end of the first week, a team of six clinicians got together to assess me, based on the 800-question inventory, plus feedback from the hospital caregivers, and from Dr. van Zandt, who was present at the session. I wasn't invited. Dr. van Zandt related to me what happened. At one point, one of the staff psychiatrists, a Dr. Pew, said, "It appears from the inventory that Mike is a very high-achieving person." He paused and continued: "It also appears very likely he will stop taking his medications as soon as he's out of the hospital, and stop seeing doctors."

After this conference, Dr. van Zandt and I met in a little conference room, just the two of us. She informed me about the observations of this Pew guy.

And now came a remarkable moment.

I got angry and defiant. Really pissed off: "How dare he?" I mean, yeah, OK, the SOB was probably right, but damn it, how dare he be right?

He had obviously hit a nerve.

I shouted to Dr. van Zandt, "I'm gonna *make* it! I'm gonna *show* him! I'm gonna do everything humanly possible to recover!

But I was flat-out scared. I felt in my heart that if I didn't commit to full recovery I would kill myself.

I believe divine intervention was a big part of this moment. I'm not saying God sticks a finger in every little thing we do but I am saying that God exists.

Fourteen years after my initial diagnosis, this meeting with Dr. van Zandt was the deciding moment for my recovery. Maybe it was the deciding moment of my life.

Around the same time, I seemed to be coming out of the worst of my pain. My increased dosage of lithium seemed to be working. (I had boosted my intake a couple of days before my admittance, at Dr. van Zandt's suggestion.) I felt blessed by this — medications usually don't work that fast. Maybe the drug's efficacy was helped by my determination to get better. Stranger things have happened in the annals of pharmacology.

So the painful part of my depression was dissipating, but I was still depressed. I wasn't out of the woods. I kept praying.

*

The days went by in a relaxed fashion. The pace at the hospital was calm. People moved slowly as they walked down the hall or ate in the dining room. (On Thanksgiving Day, about 10 days into my stay, I was allowed to leave the premises for a few hours, and I went to dinner at my parents' house. Luanne and her parents were there, too. I briefly felt disoriented, because the "real world" outside seemed to be humming along at breakneck speed!)

The hospital had several units. Mine had about 20 people. There was plenty of elbow room. They didn't want to us to feel crowded.

We lined up every morning for our medications just like in *One Flew Over the Cuckoo's Nest*. I don't think anyone got saltpeter (potassium nitrate), which is used in the movie to tamp down libidos. Jack Nicholson makes a crude joke about it in the film. (There's actually no scientific evidence that saltpeter affects the libido.)

The patients in my unit ranged in age from 18 to maybe 60 or 65. We were divided into two groups. Some of the people (all of them women) formed the "Survivors" group; they were survivors of physical or sexual abuse and/or had post-traumatic stress disorder. My group was "Mood Disorder/ Obsessive Compulsive Disorder" — men and women who had bipolar disorder, depression, schizophrenia and/or obsessive-compulsive disorder.

Therapists conducted group sessions several times each weekday. Attendance was suggested but not required. I usually went. One morning, I decided to sleep in; a staff person approached me later that day and "strongly encouraged" me to go to every session. I got the feeling that if I didn't attend every meeting, I would have to stay longer. This wasn't said to me explicitly but I caught the drift: "Stick with the program, Mike."

In group sessions, we talked about what brought us to the hospital, our fears, our aspirations, how we felt about our progress. We had to set a daily goal. Any goal was O.K. — "My goal is to say three positive things today" or "My goal is to not fall asleep during group sessions." Just like kindergarten! That said, I felt the sessions were valuable. I liked receiving focused attention from a lot of sympathetic people. Some folks spoke more than others, naturally. At one meeting, I took over a leadership role and encouraged a couple of shy people to talk. The authorities gently reminded me afterward that I wasn't there to run the sessions.

The ward was not segregated by gender. I don't think much hanky-panky was going on, but I noticed one man and one woman smooching in a corner quite often.

In addition to group sessions, we spent individual time with psychologists. This too was valuable. My psychologist was very competent. Also, we had art therapy a couple of times a week. I painted a guy rowing a boat in a stormy sea. I imagined him saying, "Hey, I'm out here in this boat, fighting all this stuff, and who knows if I'll survive." I like painting; my technique is lacking but I see a lot of feeling in my work.

We played volleyball, basketball, cards. We played Pictionary. I love Pictionary — it's a game where you identify words from drawings. It's exciting; everybody yells and gets riled up: "HOW CAN THAT BE A DOG!!!"

The hospital food was excellent: bacon and eggs, turkey sandwiches, pot roast, lasagna, baked chicken. The conversation at the dining table was always friendly.

A lot of patients watched tons of TV but I never liked doing that. I liked hanging out with people. For example:

- I became pals with Lonnie, who was in the hospital because he had brought a rifle to work and threatened to kill his boss. (Several patients were there for criminal behavior like this.) So far as I could tell, he was not the murdering type, whatever that type is. He was a nice guy. He liked basketball. He corrected my form on the court. He said, "Don't look at the ball, Mike. You know where the ball is. Look at the hoop!" I said, "Ah! Thanks Lonnie!" Meanwhile, I corrected his form in the cafeteria. When I put my napkin in my lap, he got confused. He had never seen anyone do that before.

"Why are you putting it in your lap, man?" My reply: "That's the way it's done, Lonnie." He said, "O.K., cool."

• One afternoon while I was sitting by myself at a table in the commons area, an attractive woman came over and asked me to play poker. We introduced ourselves; she said her name was Raven. We quietly played seven-card stud for a while — she was very good — and then she looked at me and said, "You wanna know something?" I said, "OK" She said, "I'm a prostitute." I said, in a neutral tone, "Oh, interesting," and tried to indicate, with my manner, "No big deal." When she saw I wasn't judging her, she opened up a little bit, talking about her pimp, and a few details of her life, such as how many clients she could accommodate in an evening's work (quite a few). I learned later that she was a famous sleepwalker in the ward. She would sleepwalk into someone's room in the middle of the night, lay down on the bed, and start yelling. I never heard her yell, nor did I get a night-time visit, but other patients gave me the scoop. The beds of strangers lured and terrified the beautiful and sad Raven.

• I usually didn't sleep very well at night. Bipolar disorder is marked by poor sleep. I joined a group of four or five bipolar guys every morning around 3 o'clock at a little nook that had vending machines with candy bars, coffee, soda pop. We would solve the problems of the world: How the election of 1992 had turned out, what sort of president Bill Clinton was going to be. The hospital staff was OK with us getting together. There was no Nurse Ratched ordering us around or anyone like that.

• A guy named Charles lived in the room next to mine.

He was in his 50s and had schizophrenia. His goal in life was to rebuild Euclid Beach Park, a famous amusement park on Lake Erie in Cleveland that opened in the 1890s and closed in 1969. I spent many fun days there as a kid in the '50s and '60s. It was family-friendly, with a roller coaster, merry-go-rounds, kiddie rides, a beautiful beach, rowboat rentals, a dance pavilion, campgrounds, a baseball field, hot dogs, soda pop, cotton candy and Humphrey popcorn balls, a local specialty. Couples went on first dates at Euclid Beach Park and got married there a few months later. The park closed down when I was 16; I guess TV killed it. Charles stayed in his room most of the time making plans for the park's resurrection. I would knock on his door and say "Hi Charles! How's the project coming along?" He saw that I was a good listener. (As I mentioned, bipolar illness can enhance empathy.) He launched into monologues about the long-lost days of Euclid Beach Park glory, showed me a scrapbook with park postcards from the 1930s, and discussed his business plan. He was all set to go; all he needed was a lot of money. (I doubt he ever got it.) As I think about Charles now, I suppose the park was a metaphor for him, a symbol of fun and youth and good times, something to cling to. As I left his room I always said, "Good luck!" He would smile and say, "See you there, Mike!" I'll never forget his shining eyes.

*

When I entered the hospital I was totally depressed and suicidal. When I left, three weeks later, I was moderately depressed and not suicidal. The severe pain was gone. I was no longer hopeless.

The place did me a lot of good. I walked out of there with a plan for recovery, a tool kit:

1. A new drug regimen that I was committed to following. For the first time in my life, I was sticking to the meds.
2. A commitment to see my doctor regularly.
3. Marriage counseling to become a better husband.
4. Regular exercise.
5. Prayer and meditation.
6. The support of Luanne.

I want to put special emphasis on Item No. 6, which was really No. 1 in terms of importance (or, let's say, tied for first with the drug regimen). Luanne is great. She held a 50-hour-a-week teaching job while I was in the hospital, visited me every other day, and fielded all the concerned phone calls from my family and friends. She listens. She's got a big heart. She's there. Her health insurance paid the medical bills.

Family support is a huge thing in recovery from mental illness. I don't believe it's absolutely essential to have family support — I think a person can manage without it — but if it's there, things probably go easier. I thank God every day for Luanne.

I want to mention one additional tool in my tool kit. I started getting better at identifying anger. As I've mentioned, that had been a challenge my whole life. I bottled my anger so tightly that I didn't even feel it. (Some people say that anger turned inward becomes depression; I think that's probably true.)

The hospital bill was $16,000. I thanked God I had good insurance.

*

I needed two years to become 100 percent of my old self. In the next chapter, I describe a key part of this journey: getting help from the 12-step concept, even though there's no 12-step group specifically for people with bipolar disorder.

CHAPTER 4

My Recovery After The Hospital With Help From Support Groups

As I walked out the door of the hospital on the chilly morning of December 7, 1992, I swore to God I'd never return. I stopped on the sidewalk just before getting into the car (my wife was driving), looked to the sky and thought, "Never again, God."

One trip down that corridor was plenty for me in this lifetime. I was open to all techniques for healing. "Whatever it takes" was my mantra.

I decided to use 12-step recovery groups.

You probably know what I mean by 12-step. This is the approach created in the 1930s by the founders of Alcoholics Anonymous to help people stop drinking. It's a systematic course of action for recovering health and fitness. Among the 12 steps: recognizing a higher power that can give strength, making amends for errors, and helping others in their quest to recover.

The 12-step concept has expanded over the years to encompass all manner of addictions and compulsions including narcotics, gambling, overeating and sex. The majority of 12-step adherents are recovering from alcohol and other drugs.

The seed for this approach was planted in me when I was in the hospital. A nurse named Betty mentioned to me that Co-Dependents Anonymous (CoDA) might be good for me after I went home. No one else at the hospital ever said anything to me along these lines — none of the doctors, none of the other nurses, just this one wise and conscious soul, whom I thank to this day. Nurses, I believe, are sometimes more in touch than doctors with practical solutions to people's problems. They're in the trenches. They're constantly on the lookout for stuff that works quickly and efficiently. Maybe they're less encumbered by textbook theory. Textbook theory has its place, but perhaps it's sometimes a bit detached from the real world.

I decided to investigate CoDA. And then I had a thought: Maybe Alcoholics Anonymous (AA) would be helpful for me too, even though I don't drink much at all. (Booze has never much interested me; I can take it or leave it.)

In all my years of dealing with bipolar disorder, no one ever suggested AA as a way to get support. I had to think it up for myself based on Betty's suggestion. Well, I'm good at finding creative solutions; if I decide to accomplish something, I'm gonna think out of the box and find a way to succeed.

I was somewhat familiar with AA. A good friend of mine, Frank, joined the group in the mid-1980s and always said it helped him change his life. I knew the basics of how things worked.

I actually visited about half-a-dozen support groups when I got out of the hospital, to check out the vibe and see if they might be useful to me. For each group, I attended three or four meetings. I visited AA, Recovery Incorporated (now Recovery International), Al-Anon, Neurotics Anonymous, the National Depressive and Manic-Depressive Association, one or two others. Each one was different; each one was good.

I went to my first AA meeting on Saturday morning, January 23, 1993, at Club 24, Room 203, 2490 Lee Boulevard in Cleveland Heights, an ordinary four-story brick office building where lots of 12-step groups met.

I walked in. A guy at the door shook my hand. People were standing around talking, laughing, connecting. I was a little bit surprised by this. I half-expected the vibe to be sort of bleak and down-in-the-dumps — "woe is me," yadda yadda. Not so. Quite the opposite.

I saw a table with coffee and doughnuts. Probably every table at every AA meeting, ever, has had coffee and doughnuts.

It's an unofficial part of the deal, apparently. I grabbed a powdered sugar doughnut and some coffee. People came over and shook my hand and said hello.

The room held about 30 people, about two-thirds men, one-third women. About half the folks were African-American and half were white. About 10 a.m. we sat down on metal folding chairs and the meeting began. I sat in the back.

The meeting had a leader, a man in his 40s who led the Lord's Prayer. Then someone else read the 12 steps out loud:

1. We admit we are powerless over alcohol, that our lives have become unmanageable.

2. We have come to believe that a power greater than ourselves can restore us to sanity.

3. We have made a decision to turn our will and lives over to the care of God as we understand him.

4. We have made a searching and fearless moral inventory of ourselves.

5. We have admitted to God, to ourselves, and to another human being the exact nature of our wrongs.

6. We are entirely ready to have God remove all these character defects.

7. We have humbly asked God to remove our shortcomings.

8. We have made a list of all the persons we have harmed and have become willing to make amends to them.

9. We made direct amends to such people whenever

possible, except when to do so would injure them or others.

10. We have continued to take personal inventory, and when we are wrong, we admit it.

11. We have sought through prayer and meditation to improve our conscious contact with God (as we understand him) praying only for knowledge of His will for us and the power to carry that out.

12. Having had a spiritual awakening as a result of these steps, we have tried to carry this message to other alcoholics, and to practice these principles in all our affairs.

I could feel the power of those words.

I'll interject a bit of history here. The noted psychiatrist and author M. Scott Peck said in an interview that the creation of AA in 1935 was "perhaps the greatest event of the 20th century." It was start of the self-help movement, Peck said, which has rippled through society in countless good ways. AA teaches people to "become more compassionate and at the same time more competent," Peck said. It teaches people to be *awake*, he continued, and appreciate life, their fellows and the environment. It teaches people about community. As more people learn about these things, "we take control of our own lives and become intolerant of irresponsible governments, of waste, of incompetent bureaucracy, of prejudice."

Remembering that AA meeting, and listening to the 12 steps being read out, feeling the love and compassion and hearing the stories of recovery, I know in my heart that Peck was 100 percent correct.

One guy stood up. He was the "lead" for the meeting — he told the story of his life. Over the course of 10 minutes, he described how booze had snuck up on him and suddenly grabbed him. I found his story to be very painful to listen to, but at the same time I could see that he was gaining something positive from standing up, speaking honestly and feeling the acceptance. He was telling people the worst about his life, really bad stuff, and they were saying, "It's OK! We love you, man!" (They were saying this in their minds; you aren't interrupted if you're a lead.)

Louis Armstrong had a hit record in 1967 called "What a Wonderful World." It has a great line: "I see friends shaking hands/Saying how do you do/But they're really saying/I love you." That was the vibe as this quiet gentleman at the meeting spoke about his life struggle.

One single meeting of AA and I got it: This organization can enhance and sustain my recovery from bipolar disorder. I related to alcoholics. They have an illness that's probably genetically based to some degree (so do I). They experienced depression and despair (so did I). They knew something about death (so did I) — they wanted to drink themselves into major problems and death; I was going to skip the middle step and go straight to death.

I'm pretty sure other bipolar people have used this magnificent resource over the years. I hope so.

I say to you: If you're bipolar, AA might be helpful That's one of the two or three most important things I'll say in this book. In my opinion, if you jump on that train, and stick to your meds, and get some exercise, you stand a pretty good chance of getting better.

You don't need to worry that the folks at AA will throw you out if they find out you're bipolar and not an alcoholic. They're not into exclusion; they're into inclusion. You don't need to get up and say anything. I never did and no one seemed to mind. I went for the warmth and high spirits and hopefulness and weekly inspiration.

AA has taken some hits over the years, and has been the butt of jokes in Las Vegas and on TV. But I felt great as I drove home that day. Researchers believe a sense of social connection can be extremely useful in achieving and preserving health, and AA says, "We're a family for you."

*

CoDA was just as important to me as AA — perhaps more so. Codependent people can be too nice. They often hold back on expressing how they feel for fear of rejection. They can do too much for others.

Have I been codependent all my life? Maybe. Maybe my turkey dinner when I was 12 years old was an early sign of it, although I'm not 100 percent sure about that — maybe the dinner was just a great thing to do. As Freud supposedly once said, "Sometimes a cigar is just a cigar." (There's not a whole lot of evidence he really said it, but you get the drift, i.e., it's not true that every single event in a person's life is fraught with big psychological weight.)

Here's another example of my codependency. When I was preparing to go to the hospital, I got Luanne's address book and copied down phone numbers of three of her close friends so that I could call them, from the hospital, and make sure she was OK.

My first CoDA gathering was in a church parish hall about two miles from my home. It unfolded in a very similar way to AA except the CoDA folks didn't use the Lord's Prayer at the start; instead, they recited the famous Serenity Prayer by theologian Reinhold Niebuhr: "God, grant me the serenity to accept the things I cannot change, courage to change the things I can, and wisdom to know the difference." (Has humanity ever produced a more profound sentence than that?)

I felt at home in CoDA. I actually got more involved with the group than with AA, going to meetings more regularly, helping more often with organizational tasks. The words "wisdom to know the difference" resonated with me as I considered whether my helpful and considerate nature

49

might also be part of an excessive desire to fix or rescue or take responsibility for others.

The movement to recognize codependency accelerated in 1986 with publication of two excellent books: *Diagnosing and Treating Co-Dependence* by Dr. Timmen Cermak and the best-selling *Codependent No More* by Melody Beattie. These books paved the way for the launch of Co-Dependents Anonymous in October of '86.

Codependency is a tricky condition. It's a lifelong illness not treatable by drugs, but improvement is definitely possible. I estimate that my codependency is about 50 percent less today than when I was in my 30s and 40s, and I attribute most or all of that improvement to my work with CoDA. I'm much more aware today of my feelings and much more willing to express them.

I've wondered over the years if my codependency is related to my bipolar disorder. I've never seen a study that correlates the two conditions, but I will note that my bipolar condition makes me super-sensitive at times, very empathetic, so yeah, maybe that fact links to my worrying excessively, at times, about what other people think.

The human brain and nervous system hold lots of mysteries. Scientists haven't figured out many of the intricacies of the brain despite spending billions of dollars over the last 50 years to track exactly how all the chemicals interact. Maybe 100 years from now we'll have a full understanding of what's what.

*

Those two years of post-hospital recovery were difficult, but I made it, with the help of those wonderful groups, my wife and family, my psychiatrist, and the other items in my tool kit. During the two years, I re-evaluated everything about my life, asking big questions: Who am I? What kind of job should I be doing? Should I be married? (Definitely yes to that one;

Luanne and I are happy.) At the end of those years I embarked on the most prolific, adventurous, creative and rewarding time of my life. I was soon able to say, "I did all this, and oh, by the way, I have a mental illness."

CHAPTER 5

My Adventures Doing Good Things For The People Of Borneo

I was invited to Singapore in the spring of 1998 by my brother Matthew and his wife, Joyce, who were employed there. I said, "Sure thing!" As a result of this trip, I became involved in the life of the neighboring island of Borneo, assisting in the building of a school, the financing of a fruit plantation and the launching of a little telephone company.

This work, the most satisfying of my life, came forth, in part, from my bipolar disorder, and from the recovery that commenced with my hospital stay. As I've indicated in previous pages, my bipolar condition stirs deep currents of creativity and empathy within me. I helped build that school in Borneo with the help of those traits. (And my capacity for hard work. And a little bit of luck.) My recovery, which began at the hospital, gave me tools for focusing and channeling the creativity and empathy.

My work in Borneo was lonely. I often wished for a guidebook, not one for tourists, but some sort of illumination on the pathway of doing good. One of my goals for this chapter is provide tips in case you get a yen to make a positive impact on the world. (The world really needs your help.)

*

I had a great time in Singapore, a rich and bustling city in Southeast Asia.

It has a population of four million — Chinese, Malays, Indians, Eurasians and other groups. It's an independent city-state. Singaporean companies specialize in turning raw materials into electronics, machinery, medical equipment and advanced plastics. When I was there, big hotels and office buildings were being built downtown.

Singapore was founded in 1819 as a trading post for the East India Company. The city was a key asset of the British Empire because of its proximity to major shipping lanes (it's known as the "Gibraltar of the East" and is one of the busiest ports in the world). Singapore gained independence in 1963.

It's known for shopping and great food. Food is a very big deal there. The fancy restaurants are some of the best in the world, and even the casual places are good. I loved the food stands on the streets where we got great meals for three or four bucks apiece — "hawker food" — fish dumplings, noodle soup, spring rolls, curried octopus on rice. My favorite restaurant was a little place called Jai Thai, where for five bucks I got incredible Pad Thai: chicken, rice noodles, eggs, tofu, vegetables, peanuts, lime wedges, fish sauce. (Beats the heck out of McDonald's cheeseburgers.)

We drank some beer, strolled around and saw the sights, including Jurong Bird Park, with 5,000-plus birds of 400 species; Singapore Botanic Gardens, with a rain forest and lush orchids; the amazing resort of Sentosa; and the ship traffic.

Then I hopped on a plane and flew 900 miles, almost due east, to Borneo.

I went to Borneo because I wanted adventure in the jungle, something off the beaten track. Bipolar people love travel and novelty (not all of us but many of us). I first got interested in Borneo in 1988 when I saw the documentary "Ring of Fire," produced by the brothers Lorne and Lawrence Blair, who had spent a decade on the vast but little-known island.

Borneo is situated on the Equator between China, to the north, and Australia, to the southeast. It's about the size of Texas. Three nations have territory in Borneo: Indonesia, Malaysia and Brunei. I was in the Indonesian section, which is known as Kalimantan.

Indonesia is a sprawling collection of islands formerly known as the Dutch East Indies. The number of islands is debated, perhaps more than 15,000. Among the best known are Bali, Java and Sumatra.

The nation is the fourth most-populous in the world, with 260 million people. It includes more than 350 ethnic groups and 700-plus languages—a "bewildering mosaic," writes journalist Pankaj Mishra. The main language is Indonesian.

Ethnic and political tensions have generated considerable violence over the years, including a terrible time in 1965–66 when hundreds of thousands of Communists and their families were slaughtered after a failed coup attempt. (Also killed and tortured during that period: union leaders, teachers, and women's rights activists. The American government supported the genocide. Indonesia has never tried to come to grips with this horror — no trials, no memorials.)

Almost 90 percent of Indonesians are Muslim. Their brand of the faith, known as Islam Nusantara or East Indies Islam, stresses nonviolence and acceptance of all major religions. Which isn't to say Indonesia hasn't had its religious problems; jihadists bombed Bali in 2002 and 2005 and Jakarta in 2016.

I did some research before leaving Cleveland and found a company called Intrepid Travel with cool tours in Borneo. The company is run by an Australian fellow named Dave Bowling. I recommend this outfit to anybody who wants a good time with a little bit of an edge — serious hiking in the rainforest and staying in the homes of local folks. To me, this is a big part of what travel is all about.

Early in the planning stages, Luanne and I discussed the trip. She was worried because of some violence that had occurred in the country. But she understands my need to travel alone occasionally and to challenge myself with a certain amount of risk. People ask her, "How can you let him go?" Her reply: "He's over 21, and my impinging on his need to go to Borneo would be a great way to build resentment in our marriage."

My biggest fear was snakes. I'm definitely afraid of poisonous snakes (I have no problem with the nonpoisonous kinds). Indonesia has lots of bad-news snakes including king cobras (which can grow to 18 feet), pythons (non-poisonous but potentially lethal) and several other species.

*

I arrived in the city of Balikpapan, Borneo, Indonesia. This is an oil and gas town adjacent to the Makassar Strait. Shell Oil has taken a lot of energy out of the strait over the years. The population of Balikpapan when I was there was about 600,000.

The city has some nice hotels, but I decided to live on the edge (kind of) by spending the night in a questionable-looking hotel (by my standards). I woke up in the morning with dozens of itchy welts on my body from flea bites. My first thought when this kind of thing happens is "Hey, it's an adventure!"

For breakfast I went out and bought food from a street vendor —chicken and vegetables with white rice (rice is served with pretty much every meal in Indonesia). I had a couple of hours to check out the neighborhood before heading for the city of Samarinda to meet my tour group. I put on my backpack (which included a big bottle of water) and started walking around.

The weather was hot and humid even in the early morning. The temperature was probably around 90; the humidity made it seem even hotter.

The streets were full of people on motor scooters and bicycles. Minibuses carried six to eight people to their jobs.

There was lots of air pollution, some of it from the traffic, much of it from slash-and-burn farming techniques many miles away.

I didn't see a single gas station and couldn't figure out where people were getting gasoline. Eventually I grasped the sales method: People stand by the road with five-gallon containers of gas, and when you run out, you buy from them. Many people seemed poor. I saw an open sewer; it had a horrible stench. I saw a couple of cats with nasty open sores. Kids begged me for money. They looked reasonably healthy, but they probably needed a good meal or two, so I gave them some change.

People stared at me as I walked around — partly, I think, because white people didn't show up in that part of town very often, partly because I was taller than most everyone on the street. I'm six feet tall; the average Indonesian man stands about 5'2" or 5'3". Many folks made eye contact with me and smiled. I smiled back.

Young Indonesian women dressed in cotton shirts and batik sarongs came up to me and said, "I love you" or "Hello, I love your blue eyes." They weren't propositioning me — at least I don't think so. They just wanted to say something nice. Maybe "I love you" was the only phrase they knew in English. They kept walking after saying hi.

I walked into a mini-mall, an enclosed shopping area, and was surrounded by half a dozen lively kids, ages 6 or 7 to about 11 or 12. They followed me around as if I were the Pied Piper of Hamlin. They wanted money but they weren't demanding about it. They quickly decided to stop begging and just hang out with me for a while. I was the best show in town, or maybe the only show they could afford. One little boy was fascinated by the hairs on my arm.

I did a little magic trick for the kids. You know that trick where you pretend you've pulled off your thumb? That went over big — I probably did it 10 times and got a chorus of laughter every time. The kids were trying to figure it out for themselves but they couldn't quite get it until I showed them. Maybe that trick is still being taught in that section of Balikpapan — "Remember the tall American? He taught us!"

I gave the kids balloons and plastic puzzles. We blew soap bubbles. I always travel with these items because they break the ice with kids, and once kids are laughing and happy, the adults jump in and want to meet me. (I hardly ever saw other Americans as equipped as I was to make kids happy; I urge this tactic to anyone who wants to feel really welcomed.) The kids and I ended up in an arcade with an air hockey game. I paid for them to play for as long as they wanted. I made sure they got their fill, for once, of air hockey. I'll never forget the sight of them crowded around that hockey table, yelling and laughing. Maybe it was the highlight of their month or year. It was a highlight of my life and it cost me next to nothing. I watched for a few minutes, left the arcade, bought an Indonesian phrase book at a bookstore and continued walking around.

I conversed with two teenage sisters and their older brother. They spoke a bit of English and I had my new phrase book, plus we had sign language, so we had a nice chat. They had seen the film *Titanic* and were singing "My Heart Will Go On." They were dressed in the fine white linen that Muslim women and girls wear. They had the same brightness of spirit of teenagers everywhere. One of the girls wanted to be a doctor. They said, excitedly, that they wanted me to meet their brothers and sisters, and indicated they would come to my hotel the next morning. I figured it wasn't likely.

Much to my surprise, I heard a knock at my door at 8:30 the next morning, and there they were, six siblings: the two girls, two additional girls (younger) and two boys (teenagers). They came in the room and we talked. I showed them pictures of my family. We exchanged addresses. It was very pleasant. They didn't want anything from me, just the chance to say hello and meet an American.

I want to point here a basic fact of travel: America really matters to people in other countries. Not to all of them, of course, but to a lot of them. We in the U.S. lose sight of how much our country matters internationally. I believe that many young people in Indonesia greatly admire America, that we symbolize opportunity, freedom and friendliness. People in other countries may not always like our government, but they often like us as individuals if we're willing to walk among them and smile and look approachable. When I'm overseas I think of myself as an American ambassador. I'm almost always smiling. I got a cab in the early afternoon and we drove north to Samarinda, two and a half hours from Balikpapan. I paid the taxi driver the equivalent of about $15 for the trip. He was delighted with his payday. A skilled worker in that area might make a dollar a day; teachers make about $2 a day.

Samarinda is located on the banks of the Mahakam River. The population at that time was about 750,000. At the hotel, I met up with my tour group: the two guides, Dave, the trip leader, from Australia, and Alex, an Indonesian; and Vicki and Richard, who were traveling together. I had expected more people in the group; I was pleasantly surprised by the small number. They were nice folks with a quest for adventure. We had an early dinner and got acquainted.

*

After dinner I heard gorgeous chanting from the speakers of a minaret. It was an Islamic call to prayer, the *adhan*, which occurs five times daily. It was beautiful, mystical, eerie — some of the loveliest singing I had ever heard. I was intrigued and asked at my hotel for the location of the nearest mosque, got directions, and started walking there.

Prayer time, *salat*, was over by the time I got there. The mosque was deserted but the doors were open. The building seemed welcoming to a lonely visitor from America.

I had never been in a mosque before but I knew enough to take off my shoes before entering the prayer hall. The hall was very clean and comfortable. There were no chairs or benches, just carpets, presumably facing toward Mecca. Shelves were lined with books.

I kneeled, bent forward and prayed a nondenominational

prayer. I trust it was heard by my God. I said to myself, "The God of all religions is the same God."

I grew up Catholic, as I mentioned earlier. I was an altar boy and attended a Catholic high school. I don't make a big noise about it, but yeah, God has a place in my life. I felt honored and blessed to be praying in this holy place, a serene refuge from the noise and grime of the city. I prayed for peace in the world and for a safe trip. I thanked God for helping me get healthy. When I finished, as I made my exit, I admired the building's pastel-colored walls and graceful curves and thought of the many hundreds of years of history of this great religion.

When I got back to my hotel, walking through the lobby, I came upon a group of about 15 young Indonesian men who were being trained by Kubota, a big Japanese company, in tractor maintenance. They smiled and I smiled; we chatted a bit. One man asked me, "Are you Muslim?" I said, "No." And then I repeated, out loud, my thought from a few minutes earlier: "The God of all religions is the same God." They nodded very appreciatively.

I showed them the pictures of my family. When they saw my beautiful niece Angie, age 24, they flipped out. They wanted her address to write to her!

I was impressed by these fellows and thought, "Kubota has some good employees here, and Indonesia has some good citizens." There's a large historical irony here. During World War II, Japan occupied the Dutch East Indies including Borneo. Many Indonesians suffered and were killed. Slave labor was common. Here, in this lobby, Japan and Indonesia found something akin to peaceful common ground. In this brief encounter, I found solid evidence that the world can get better.

The evening affected me deeply. I should mention something else. Before embarking on the trip, and with the understanding of my doctor, I stopped my medications temporarily, because I knew I would be backpacking in a hot, humid environment and the drugs might cause me

59

problems with the balance of salt, lithium, and water in my body. Stopping the drugs allowed me to fully experience my emotions — intense pleasure, sharp sadness, strong spirituality. Everything in Borneo seemed so powerful, emotional, awful, happy, educational, informative, rich, real. I got to my room and started crying as I thought about the poverty of the city. When I'm on my medicines I can't have a good cry, but now the tears really came.

You see things about developing countries on TV but you don't get the full message until you're there: the pain of poverty, the noxious air, the hopefulness of young people.

The crying felt good. I lay on my bed and felt the glory and pain of life. I felt the warmth of these beautiful people and I felt incredible love for America, my home, halfway around the world. I felt as much love for America at that moment as I ever have in my life.

I thanked God for letting me connect to the world.

And I asked God to help me find a way to help these people.

*

Late that evening, our tour group went to a club in Samarinda that played Indonesian dance music with a heavy disco beat. Somebody must have put the volume dial at "10." I wasn't really enjoying myself all that much; the music was just too loud and the room was filled with cigarette smoke. I was thinking about leaving when a young woman came up to me and asked for a light.

I knew what this meant. I had been forewarned by Dave and Alex, our guides. It's an aspect of the mating ritual in this part of Indonesia. It's the woman's task to make the first move by asking for a light. If the man is interested, he smiles and says, "Sure," lights her cigarette, and asks her if she would care to dance. She then says yes or no ("ya" or "tidak" in

Indonesian), depending on how she feels about his manners, his smile and his vibe.

On the other hand, if the man says, "Sorry, no, I don't have a light," that means he's not interested, and she saves face, because after all, she just wanted a light for her cigarette, she didn't want to marry the guy, right? So it's a nice formalized procedure that fits well with the Muslim culture. You see a lot of cigarettes being lit. Smoke shrouds the dance floor. If you don't smoke, and don't have a lighter, and a hot babe comes up to you and you're interested, the thing to do is to make a big deal about finding a lighter from someone.

When this woman asked me for a light, I smiled, borrowed a lighter from Alex, lit her cigarette and asked her to dance. She paused for a moment, looked me over one more time and said, "Ya." I'm not crazy about dancing but I felt I had to ask her. It seemed the polite thing to do, and after all, I was an American ambassador. We danced a couple of dances, I thanked her, we shook hands, and I headed back to my group. She followed me, pulled up a chair, and sat down next to me. My group left shortly after that, and she smiled and waved a warm farewell.

*

The next day, our group traveled up the Mahakam River, four hours by four-wheel-drive vehicle and five hours by 14-foot motorized canoe.

The 600-mile river is the main route from the coast (the Makassar Strait) to the Bornean interior and the ancient rainforest. Where we started the river was quite wide, about three football fields; when we got upriver it narrowed to 50 yards.

The river is lined with shacks, and lots of folks waved at us. Women bathed in the river while wrapped in sarongs. A man washed two children with thick soap.

That night, our group stayed with a Muslim family that

lived on the river, or I should say, over the river—a one-room shack built on stilts over the water.

The mom and dad, Utari and Bejo, were in their 30s and had five young children. Bejo was a fisherman, and Utari kept the house, cooked the food and raised the kids. The house was neat and clean. The kids were healthy and cheerful. They didn't have TV or video games or even a phone yet seemed very happy. (I wonder if there's a connection there?)

Utari made a delicious dinner of grilled small fish (caught in the river; similar to sardines), local vegetables and white rice, with a hot pepper paste known as sambal, an Indonesian specialty. She made sambal by sautéing chili peppers, tomatoes and shallots in palm oil, adding a bit of sugar, and mashing up the mixture in a mortar and pestle. Some people add other ingredients including lime juice, shrimp paste or vinegar, but she kept it simple. The key to good sambal is getting the ingredients balanced just right, otherwise it's too hot or too sugary. This sambal seemed perfect to me. Utari also served excellent hot tea in small clear glasses.

I paid about 35 cents for all this great food and overnight accommodations. I wanted to give them a tip, but the money situation was complicated. The tour guides cautioned us against offering tips, or flashing a lot of money, because it would disrupt the delicate unwritten balance in the tourism economy.

Other differences were apparent, too. In America we have "the pursuit of happiness" as part of our national creed, but much of the world doesn't think that way. I would guess that the main goal of these parents was to get through the day without a disaster, without one of their kids drowning in the river or getting bitten by a cobra slithering in from the jungle. What they wanted most in life, I believe, was for their children to get some education and get a secure job with a good company, like Kubota, Nike, General Motors, Coca-Cola, Bank Mandiri, Astra International, or HM Sampoerna. And marry well and produce grandchildren.

(Nike is a big deal in Indonesia, employing more than 100,000 people. I saw a lot of Nike signs in the cities.)

After supper that evening, the kids squealed with delight when I did magic tricks and we blew soap bubbles. I gave them balloons, which they played with for many minutes. The bright colors of the balloons stood out. Vivid colors were somewhat lacking in that environment; the clothes and furnishings were fairly monochromatic.

Soap bubbles. Balloons. I don't want to get all sentimental about the "simple pleasures," but I will say, those kids looked as happy as can be playing with these modest items.

I now need to mention something rather unpleasant. The Mahakam River was full of human excrement. Each house on the river has an outhouse. Hundreds of outhouses extended upriver for many miles. Shit goes straight into the river from the outhouses. The river was awful (and still is) even though the waste is broken down fairly quickly by bacteria. Families boil river water before drinking it, of course, but I can't help but worry about how they might be affected by cholera and other diseases. (Our tea was made from river water. This made me a little nervous but I felt it was probably O.K. Also, I had gotten a slew of vaccinations before embarking on the trip.)

Mercury was also a problem in the river. Gold miners upstream used a lot of mercury in their process. (The mercury binds to gold, forming an amalgam, which is heated; this vaporizes the mercury and leaves behind gold.) The residue, including mercury, floats downstream. The official name for this work is "artisanal and small-scale mining" (ASM); it's more worrisome than human waste in terms of impact on human health. I did a bit of research on mercury after I got home. It's incredibly toxic to the nervous system. A tiny bit of mercury can pollute a lot of river water. There are significant levels of mercury in Indonesian fish, according to a study by the World Wildlife Fund.

Sadly, many millions of people in dozens of countries are engaged in ASM and are exposed to mercury, including women and children. It's possible to do small-scale mining without mercury, if people are given access to the right materials and equipment.

We Americans lose sight of a basic fact about the developing world: It's badly polluted. The people most affected by the pollution are not informed about the danger by the authorities, or choose to stay uninformed because they can't do much about it, they're just trying to survive.

Our group departed the next morning. The children lined up and waved us off, shining and happy in the morning sun. I didn't get to know this lovely family well, but I do feel I gained useful knowledge about a way of life different from my own, its beauty and its challenges.

*

We proceeded upriver in a canoe taxi propelled by a small Honda outboard steered by a driver. The motor was extremely rackety because the driver had removed the muffler to save gas. He was clearly hard of hearing; many canoe drivers suffer from hearing loss because they sit next to loud motors every working day.

The river had many bends and curves. Houses on stilts lined the banks. Boats of all shapes and sizes went past us.

After a couple of hours we reached a small village and were greeted by a troupe of children. We got ourselves ready and embarked on a five-day backpacking trek through the rainforest.

The forest was gorgeous. I felt like I was in heaven. Monkeys chattered as we hiked along a path that was probably used by Paleolithic hunters. Ancient trees formed a thick canopy overhead with shards of sunlight coming through. A thick layer of leaves and shrubs covered the ground. The flowers were incredible. Fast-moving streams flowed over boulders.

Snakes quickly slithered away from anywhere near our path. Polite snakes! Amazing!

We had a special guide for this segment of the trip, a young man named Wahtang, who was of the Dayak ethnic group. My most distinct memory of him is that he used a rock for a pillow; apparently he was accustomed to sleeping this way. Also, he insisted on sleeping right next to the fire at night, with extra wood nearby, because he was nervous about what might come out of the forest in the wee hours. (This gave me pause at first. I had no desire to wake up to the growling of a king cobra. But Dave and Alex said that Wahtang was highly superstitious; his main fear was ghosts rather than snakes. And besides, said Dave and Alex, cobras are very shy toward humans. Good to know.)

I carried a 34-pound pack with a first-aid kit. I was prepared for emergencies, just like a Boy Scout. My feeling about risk is, I like it, but I also prefer to reduce it whenever possible. I've done a lot of backpacking in my life and I've got a list of all the essential things to carry, including water purification tablets and really good mosquito netting, which, oddly enough, no one else on this trip had. They slathered on repellant and squished down into their sleeping bags to avoid getting bitten.

The water tablets came in handy. I drank two gallons of water a day in the jungle. Eventually, everybody started using my tablets.

We came to a village. We met a young mother, about 18 years old, and her son, who was maybe 2. His shoulder had a large open sore, a skin ulcer as big as my hand. He may have had had a fever. I'm not sure if the wound was infected or not, but it didn't look good, and the mom was worried. She asked, through Alex and Wahtang, if we had anything that might help. I thought, "I'm no doctor." I had given my tube of antibiotic ointment to Utari and Bejo. The only thing I had was a tube of cortisone cream; maybe this would help but it could possibly make it worse. She seemed desperate for something, so I gave her the tube along with instructions translated through Alex and Wahtang: "Try a tiny little bit first on the corner of the wound. If it gets worse, stop using it right away."

I felt bad for that young mommy and her little boy. For them to get medical attention, they would have to travel for a day, on foot, to reach a village that had a motor scooter, then ride the motor scooter to a place where they could get a bus, and pray they could find a doctor or clinic, which are very scarce in that region. If they could find a doctor or nurse, a few pennies worth of antibiotic would probably clear that thing right up—but it was a big "if." I think often of that young mom, so worried, and the little boy watching us with his big dark eyes.

The river was about 15 yards wide in that area. It was clean, so we went swimming for about 20 minutes, at which point Wahtang suddenly signaled to us to get out of the water. A huge python was loitering about 25 yards away. It seemed to be as big as a medium-size tree. It wasn't after us, necessarily. It was probably watching for one of the monkeys, up in the trees, to fall into the water while swinging across to the opposite bank. Still, better safe than sorry; we got out.

At the end of the hike we visited an orangutan reserve. This was heartbreaking in a way, but also encouraging.

There's a big illegal international trade in exotic pets, and many Bornean orangutans are caught by it. Poachers shoot the moms and kidnap the babies for selling to rich people (Indonesians, Taiwanese, etc.) who want a conversation piece in their living rooms. Some of the poachers get caught with the goods. These little orangutans find new homes in reserves (if, that is, they survive the trauma of losing mommy and being put in a cage; many don't). I decided to take the a positive approach to this continuing tragedy. I found it encouraging that humans were putting so much effort into helping these little critters.

I was walking along a path in the reserve when an adolescent orangutan came toward me and stuck out its long arm as if it wanted to shake my hand. I extended my hand in friendship. It climbed up on me; it wanted to be held. I was happy to oblige.

I had never seen an orangutan close-up before; now I was carrying one along a path in a rainforest. My new friend was beautiful with that orange-red fur and those intelligent eyes. He or she (I'm not sure which) had a wistful, slightly melancholy expression. Maybe I felt some empathy with the wistfulness. It had incredibly long fingers; gripping power for climbing. I've heard that each orangutan finger has the strength of a man's hand.

Orangutans are the only great apes in Asia. They have 96.4 percent of human genes. They reproduce very slowly; females give birth to one infant every four or five years. Their last wild habitat, in Borneo and Sumatra, is rapidly disappearing, as people cut down rainforest and create palm oil plantations (many of which are illegal). This process has become one of the leading causes of rainforest destruction. Plenty of organizations are fighting this, but they face an uphill battle. The world loves palm oil.

The Rainforest Action Network has a fact sheet on palm oil[4] at its website. Another good source for information about the Indonesian environment is the organization Down to Earth. The World Wildlife Fund is doing good work. I also want to mention an Indonesian biologist named Rudi Putra, who is on the front lines trying to save the Bornean rainforest. He won the Goldman Environmental Prize in 2014. He's a hero.

*

I met a man named Rizaldy toward the end of our backpacking trip, and from this encounter sprang my involvement in the creation of a school, a fruit plantation and a telephone company.

We met in the village of Kota Bangun. But before I talk about Rizaldy, I'd like to describe what else we saw in the village.

It's occupied by about 200 Dayak people. The Dayaks are a major ethnic group on Borneo composed of many subgroups. We visited the village to check out Dayak culture, including weaving by village women, and to buy a few things. We spent the night there and felt very welcomed. We quickly learned about something else the Dayaks are famous for: headhunting.

Centuries ago, the Dayaks were among the most enthusiastic headhunters in human history. They sliced off the heads of their enemies with parang machetes, removed the skin and brains, and kept the skulls as symbols of triumph and power. They believed that if you own a person's skull, that person will be your slave in the afterlife. Headhunting mostly faded away among the Dayak tribes during the 19th century but it has cropped up a couple of times since then. During World War II, the Dayaks used headhunting in an effort to strike terror in Japanese occupiers. In the 1960s, in the huge anti-Communist terror, the Dayaks probably did some headhunting against ethnic Chinese Indonesians. The Dayaks may also have used headhunting in the 1990s and early 2000s when they ruthlessly attacked the Madurese people.

The people of this village looked calm and nonviolent, but I'll tell you what, you didn't want to be a member of the Madurese ethnic group in a Dayak village during a forced resettlement in 2001. (I'll note for the record, the Dayak taste for headhunting has been shared by lots of soldiers over the course of history, including a few Americans in Vietnam.)

The folks in the village didn't talk much about their dark past, but they don't mind making a bit of money from it. I bought an antique parang machete from a guy in a shop. It has a 15-inch blade with two little curls engraved in it. One of the local people, a teenager who spoke English, admired my new parang, and I asked him, "What are these curls for?" He said, "Make curl when you cut off head. Two heads, two curls." He paused and added, "Room for more." We both laughed.

*

Rizaldy was about 25 years old. He had just one name, in common with many Indonesians. His ethnic heritage was Dayak. He was headed home to the town of Mancong after a year at a Catholic seminary on the island of Sumatra. He had quit the school abruptly, deciding that the life of a priest wasn't for him.

We met on the stoop of a hotel on a beautiful sunny morning and chatted about our lives for a few minutes. We managed to connect despite the fact that his English wasn't great and my Indonesian was nonexistent (except for what I looked up in my handy phrase book). I guess I have a bit of a knack for connecting with people despite language barriers.

Suddenly Rizaldy blurted out his big dream: to establish a cocoa plantation and create employment for his community. He said "cocoa beans" and "jobs" with great emphasis and enthusiasm. He drew a little map for me of the area. He explained that most of the world's cocoa is grown on small family-owned farms.

I quickly got his drift, and really, his idea sounded good. Cocoa is a primary ingredient of chocolate, and the world surely loves chocolate. Indonesia grows a lot of cocoa beans; the climate is perfect. Your basic Hershey bar might very well have Indonesian cocoa in it.

Most important to me, Rizaldy seemed like the kind of guy who could get the job done. He had an aura about him — he was smart, he had energy and charisma, and he seemed to really want to help people. I trusted him. I wanted to help.

I like improving people's lives. It's an empathy thing. And I like supporting people who can improve the lives of others if they're given a bit of wherewithal. I said to Rizaldy, "When I get home to America, I'll do some research about cocoa production and send it to you." He was thrilled. Doing serious research was extremely difficult for him. I got his snail mail address and gave him my business card with my email address on it.

*

My tour group swung back to the city of Samarinda, traveling by boat. We had a final farewell dinner, toasted one another's health, and went our separate ways. I caught a plane in Jakarta and went home. As I walked in the front door on May 11, 1998, Luanne's first words to me were, "You survived! I'm glad!"

On a scale of one to 10, I'd rate the trip a definite 10. I fell in love with Indonesia—the people, the food, the sambal, the orangutans, the vibe. Even the snakes.

I resumed my life. My job at that time was as a technology commercialization consultant, determining possible applications for new processes and products. I researched cocoa and mailed Rizaldy a packet of data — how much water the plants need, the best kinds of fertilizer to use, how much a metric ton of cocoa beans sells for in the wholesale market.

One day in the middle of June I read in The Wall Street Journal that Goldman Sachs was working with the Indonesian government to offer common stock in Telkom Indonesia, the big phone company. Any article about Indonesia was going to grab my interest — after all, I'd been there, and I had felt the hopeful and energetic vibe of the place. Here, I thought, was an interesting investment opportunity. I researched the stock and bought 1,000 shares at $5 apiece. By the fourth quarter of that year, the stock was trading at $14 dollars a share, and I was pretty happy about the $9,000 profit.

One day in November, out of the blue, I received an email from a man named Eduardus, who introduced himself as the business partner of Rizaldy. The message said "Hello Mike!" and continued, "Enclosed is a business plan!" Attached to the email was a document: "A Business Proposal." I thought, "Wow, great, the cocoa plantation is really going to happen!"

I soon realized that these guys had something else in mind. They wanted me to invest $5,400 in a durian plantation.

My natural first question was, "A what?"

The durian, I learned, is "the king of fruits" in the minds of many Indonesians, Malaysians, Thais, Filipinos, Japanese and Vietnamese. It's native to Southeast Asia. It grows on beautiful big trees. A durian is heavy (up to six or seven pounds) and has a thorny husk. It drops to the ground when ripe — you want to careful when walking under a durian tree at certain times of the year because you never know when a fruit will come plummeting.

As I read the business plan, I remembered seeing people in Singapore eating durian for dessert, with gusto, as if it was frozen custard.

One British writer compares the taste and texture of durian to "a rich custard highly flavored with almonds" with overtones of "cream-cheese, onion-sauce, sherry-wine, and other incongruous dishes." The writer continues, "The more you eat of it the less you feel inclined to stop." (I myself don't like the taste, but millions of people do. It can be found in the U.S. in Asian markets.)

Here's a weird aspect to this fruit: Many durian species have awful odors. One writer describes the aroma of a certain species as "pig-shit, turpentine and onions, garnished with a gym sock." Another compares a durian repast to "eating sweet raspberry blancmange in the lavatory." It smells so bad that it's against the law to bring it on a bus. Entrances to hotels say "NO DURIAN."

The bottom line about durian is, millions of people will pay good money for it. The proposal that I got from Rizaldy and Eduardus said that durian was a better bet for their region than cocoa (they said they'd maybe branch out into cocoa at some later date). Their goal was to raise 200 durian saplings into full-grown trees and harvest fruit in six years, by 2004. They wanted to focus on the most desirable species, durian *sitokong*. They projected strong sales, a steady income, and plenty of job creation. They said I would get an equity share in the company. They earmarked a percentage of profits to be used toward scholarships for children (nice touch).

The only potential problem I saw was drought. Durian trees need lots of moisture; if the rains didn't come, the whole thing would be wrecked. We recognized, up front, that this might happen.

I said to Luanne, "Well, I don't really know these guys well, but Rizaldy seemed solid, and they're only asking for $5,400, which is less than the profit I could make on the Telkom stock if I sold it." The way I figured it, I never would have bought the stock if I hadn't gone to Indonesia; the profit felt like found money to me.

I liked the idea of giving something back to a country I had learned to love. I feel we Americans have a big responsibility toward the rest of the world. The U.S. is like a big vacuum cleaner sucking everything up. We're rich; a lot of the world's citizens are poor. I would like to see things get evened out a little bit.

I decided to investigate further.

*

This, then, was my first venture into micro-development: Small-scale help for people in developing countries in the form of modest loans, advice and labor. A micro-development project might, for example, funnel $1,000 to a small village in India for the purchase of chlorine for water, to fight diarrhea, and bed nets, to counter malarial mosquitoes.

One of the best books I've found about micro-development is *Poor Economics: A Radical Rethinking of the Way to Fight Global Poverty* (2011) by Abhijit V. Banerjee and Esther Duflo, economists at MIT (their website is pooreconomics. com). They write:

> It is possible to make very significant progress against the biggest problem in the world today (poverty) through the accumulation of a set of

small steps, each well thought out, carefully tested, and judiciously implemented. This might seem self-evident (but) it is not how policy usually gets made. If we could give up the lofty goals and empty promises (of huge macro-development projects like dams) and focus all our energies on the concrete steps we are able to take here and now to improve the lives of the poor worldwide, we would bring some real comfort to the lives of millions. ... A sense of possibility and a little bit of well-targeted help (a piece of information, a little nudge) can sometimes have surprisingly large effects. ... A push on the right lever can make a huge difference, but it is often difficult to know where the lever is.

Banerjee and Duflo point toward where levers are.

The journalist Austin Bay writes that micro-development is the "hottest buzz" in developmental aid:

Micro-development is demonstrably effective for helping build the local human infrastructure necessary to support positive, long-term economic growth. The Grameen Bank is an exemplary "micro" advocate. [It's a Nobel Peace Prize–winning micro-finance bank founded in Bangladesh in 1976.] It provides economically creative individuals and communities with low-cost loans and advice. It emphasizes individual accountability and integrity. Changes wrought by "micros" may be small, but they are victories of verifiable substance and build a human base for "macro-development" success. Micro mounts up.

*

73

I kept in touch with Alex, one of the guides on my tour. I emailed him in late 1998 and asked him to hire a canoe, go up the river and check out Rizaldy and Eduardus. I paid him $200 (a fortune for him). He did a great job, living with them for a week, asking lots of questions and sending me a complete written report with photos. His opinion was, these guys were on-the-level, rarin' to go, ready to put a lot of sweat equity into the durian project.

I worked with Rizaldy and Eduardus for four months, via email, to refine their business plan. I asked tough questions and got good answers. I wanted this business to succeed — for them, not for me — so I held their feet to the fire and demanded rigorous planning at every step: where will you buy your seeds? How often will you need to visit the plantation? How will you transport the durian to market?

Meanwhile I obtained a commitment for $3,600 from the Jakarta office of Catholic Relief Services, working with a very helpful woman named Yenni Suryani. (I thought Rizaldy and Eduardus were Muslim, as are more than 85 percent of Indonesians, but they turned out to be Catholic.)

During these months, I worried a bit about whether I was being codependent. As I've discussed in a previous chapter, a codependent person has trouble saying "no" and goes overboard in the direction of pleasing or helping another person. It's self-sacrifice carried to an extreme. I decided that in this situation, codependency didn't apply. I felt that my work for Rizaldy and Eduardus was a healthy and legitimate extension of my life-long interest in helping poor people around the world. It felt to me like a mission, a good one. It felt like strong empathy rather than burdensome codependency.

In early 1999, I wired half the money, $2,700, to my two associates, and I sent another big check pretty soon thereafter. Then another check. And another. I invested about $10,000 in durian. I didn't expect to get the money back.

This, as it turned out, was wise.

I'm sorry to report that the durian plantation didn't make it. The reason: drought.

Indonesia was hit by a drought in the 2000s caused by El Niño, the famous weather pattern of the Pacific Ocean that affects global rainfall and temperatures. Our durian trees grew like gangbusters from 2000 to 2003, but in '04 they suddenly dried up like kindling on a hot day in Arizona. They could not be saved. We were very disappointed, needless to say.

But all things considered, the durian plantation was a useful learning experience. I gained knowledge about planning a business via email, checking people out, financing and keeping expectations to a reasonable level. These things paved the way for the phone company and the school.

*

The phone company idea emerged in the spring of 2000.

The durian plantation was a going concern during those months. I decided to revisit Indonesia, get to know Rizaldy better, meet Eduardus, hang out with Alex, and check out our trees.

I flew to Balikpapan in early May. This trip took 50 hours: Cleveland to Minneapolis to Tokyo to Singapore to Balikpapan. I stayed overnight in Balikpapan. We were scheduled to meet Rizaldy and Eduardus in the village of Mancong, up the river another 50 miles. This part of the trip took five hours by SUV and another five hours by motorized canoe. We encountered repeated delays. For instance, the SUV driver ran out of gas, and no one was standing by the side of the road with a five-gallon container. Alex and I sat for three hours while the driver hiked to the next village. We expected to arrive in Mancong in early morning but didn't get there until late afternoon.

I came bearing gifts. I had a large box full of pens, pencils, wind chimes made in Vermont, hair-care products for the women and girls, clothing, and several dozen toothbrushes donated by my dentist. I had assembled these items back in the States after getting advice from Rizaldy and Eduardus about what to bring. I carried that big box through a bunch of airport concourses. If I were doing the trip over again, I'd mail the thing. One more lesson learned.

Alex and I stepped off the boat in Mancong and were escorted toward the center of the village. We went up over a little hill, and whoa, what's this? At least 100 of the village's 300 residents started cheering! They were my official greeters. They stood on the main street, in front of a longhouse, dressed in gorgeous ceremonial regalia. I was blown away by the big turnout. I kept thinking, "How long have they been waiting for me in this heat in their best clothes?" (About four hours, I'd guess.)

Rizaldy and Eduardus were standing in the crowd. We all hugged as if we were family.

A ceremony of greeting now commenced, conducted by a fierce-looking guy who wore a boar's tooth necklace and did a lot of yelling. His job was to make sure I was worthy of being admitted to the village. He bellowed "Teman atau musuh?" (Alex translated: "Friend or foe?") I answered "Friend!" ("Teman!") The fierce guy nodded. He gave me a parang. I used it to cut a vine to officially enter the village. Everyone cheered. I asked Alex, "What if I had said 'foe'?" He replied, "They cut head off" and laughed.

The villagers sat me down and painted my face white. Ceremonial dances began, about 20 young women in traditional costumes, doing very complex movements that involved feet, legs, arms, torso, hands, neck, head and eyes. They were accompanied by a six-piece ensemble that played drums and gongs.

Once again I thought, "How long have they been waiting?" I also said to myself, "I don't deserve this attention." I felt overwhelming happiness and a fair bit of unworthiness; I wanted to cry. I controlled this impulse pretty well but a few tears came down my face. (While I write these words, as I think about those sweet smiles, I'm getting teary. These folks treated me as if I was their long-lost beloved brother.)

I applauded the harvest dance, rice bowl dance, gong dance, shaman dance, warrior dance and chasing-away-evil-spirits dance.

I was handed a blow gun, five feet long, and invited to shoot a dart at a fake animal, made of vines, about 50 feet away. I thought, "O.K., I can do this, I'm a trumpet player!" I took a deep breath and fired. I hit the target — bravo! — but the dart bounced off.

People looked at me with stunned faces. Uh-oh. Had I done something taboo? Had I brought seven years of bad luck? I tried another shot. The dart stuck and everyone smiled. I was their brother again.

They asked me to dance and sing a solo. I danced a few modest steps and sang "I Can See Clearly Now." Everyone applauded. I was overwhelmed.

Now began the banquet. They cooked fish and chicken over an open fire and sang more songs. Fifty people attended; I felt a little bit sorry for the villagers who weren't invited. Kids peeked in through the windows.

We exchanged gifts. I received a beautiful hand-carved wooden bowl. I handed out the stuff I'd brought. Everyone was thrilled with my presents; I completely forgot about how much that box weighed as I hauled it through airports. If you ever visit Borneo, keep in mind that a few pens and bottles of shampoo go a long way. If you bring wooden chimes from Vermont, you might get elected chief.

*

We visited the durian plantation a few days later. The trees were coming along fine.

The next day, Rizaldy, Eduardus and I tooled around the river. Rizaldy casually mentioned that the government had approved construction of a small phone system in the area. The villages in the region were not in great shape in terms of communications. There were no phones and there was no postal delivery. The nearest phones and post offices were many miles away. A phone system would do wonderful things for people's welfare. Folks would be able to consult with doctors. Business people could easily order supplies from wholesalers. Parents would be able to find out how their kids in the big city were faring.

The proposed phone system, said Rizaldy, was called a "wartel" and would be built by Telkom Indonesia (coincidentally, the same firm I had invested in). A truck would haul a big satellite dish to the village; workers would set it up and put a fence around it. Local people would build a 10- by 10-foot room with three booths and a switchboard. You go into one of the booths and make a call, and a dot-matrix printer gives you a bill, which you pay on the spot. It's a highly efficient turn-key system.

The setup would cost $3,000. Rizaldy was organizing the project and obtaining financing in return for a piece of the profits. He didn't have the full $3K; he was asking his relatives for contributions. He didn't ask me to participate; he apparently felt I had already done plenty for the community. Nonetheless I volunteered to help by lending them some of the cash. I saw this as a natural next step in my micro-development effort. I saw that the wartel would (a) easily eclipse the durian trees in terms of profits, and (b) get rolling a lot sooner.

Rizaldy didn't want my money at first but finally said "Oke" (i.e., "OK")

I put up $1,400 and Rizaldy got the thing built. I felt great about that. I was confirmed in my belief that Rizaldy was a solid citizen and a good man. I said to myself, "I'm not investing in telephones and durian fruit, I'm investing in a man with a vision."

The phone booths helped the local villages for a good 10 years until the arrival of cellphones and antennas. Rizaldy became known as a doer of good deeds and a man with connections, and thus got elected to the district government. He made a hefty profit from the wartel. However, years passed before my $1,400 loan was fully repaid. Rizaldy finally paid me $500, and Eduardus paid me $900. Rizaldy said he would reimburse Eduardus but I'm not certain he ever did. I hold Rizaldy in high regard. He told me I was part of his family. I felt he was sincere in his desire to help people, and I'm pleased he was successful in that regard. When I was with him in 2002 and '03, he said I totally changed his life — I made him wealthy, famous and powerful in his community.

All that said, he sort of excluded me from his life. He never once sent me an email thanking me. I learned to accept that, but this process took me a few years, and frankly it still causes me a little bit of pain. I mention it here just in the interest of saying that micro-development can get complicated.

(Eduardus was miles ahead of Rizaldy in expressing gratitude. He still keeps in touch with me by email.)

Paying back loans may not be a high priority for some Indonesians. The nation's political and business systems are full of graft. For example, an article in the *Economist* from 2015 carried this headline: "Corruption in Indonesia: A Damnable Scourge." The article says, "Indonesians of all stripes gripe about sticky-fingered officials. America's Commerce Department says foreign and domestic businesses in Indonesia regard corruption and ineffective courts as 'serious problems.'"

A little skimming off the top may be a cost of doing business in Indonesia. I intend to ask Rizaldy about this. I'm planning a hiking trip to New Zealand; I'm going to stop off in Borneo and have a conversation with these guys.

*

I became interested in the school project in 2001. Village elders in Tanjung Isuy, near Mancong, heard about me, asked Rizaldy for my email address, and contacted me about a small school they had started in their village, the first high school in the area. It didn't have a building; it used the facilities of a public grade school.

The villagers needed $30,000 to build their own facility. Could I make a contribution?

I checked them out. It was a private school. It had 13 students. It was nondenominational; students were Christian and Muslim. I agreed to try to raise money.

Rizaldy was quite heavily involved in this project so I knew it would have a lot of energy behind it. He always liked looking good in the eyes of his fellow villagers, and being associated with me helped him in that regard.

I made brochures, sending them to my friends and acquaintances, asking them to talk up my cause. I raised $1,800 and wired it over. That was enough for the villagers to buy six acres of land and lots of school supplies.

The Indonesian government now sat up and took notice. Some bureaucrat in Jakarta or Samarinda recognized that this venture had potential, saw that the elders were serious, and financed the building of a three-room schoolhouse. Pretty good, eh? Micro-development can generate leverage.

I next started raising money for desks, pencils, pens, paper, books and rulers. I raised $3,500 in this round. I asked people to donate via a check or credit card payment to International Partners in Mission (IPM), a well-run nonprofit that worked out all the details for getting the money to the right people. I recommend IPM if you're interested in micro-development and don't want to mess around with endless paperwork (www.ipmconnect.org).

I was disappointed that I couldn't do more to raise money. I have a theory about this. I believe Americans are more committed to donating to South America and Africa than to Indonesia — they hardly know where Indonesia is, nor do they know much of anything about it. I showed maps of the country to potential donors, pointed out Borneo, and described my project, but people didn't seem to connect with the place.

People turned me down for various reasons. "Oh, I already gave my limit to charity for this year." "Oh, I prefer to give to U.S. charities." And of course, "Let me get back to you about that." I approached a couple of really rich people I know; I had high hopes, but they were reluctant because, they said, their attorney told them they couldn't deduct the donation from their taxes. (Their attorney was wrong.) Finally I said to one of these rich guys, "Just give me $20 and that'll buy five chairs." He came through. Wow. Great. Thanks.

One of the challenges of micro-development, I learned, is dealing with anger at cheap people!

I went to Indonesia for a third time in 2008. I wanted to see the school. The structure was about half-built and looked solid. The school had 45 students even though the building wasn't finished yet (the kids temporarily used another structure). The villagers were very happy to see me again and the students were all smiles.

The school had 75 students by 2004 and today the number is north of 200.

*

I feel deep satisfaction about these projects. I sometimes think I got more benefit from this work than my Indonesian friends.

It's intensely rewarding, in a spiritual sense, to do service, to help others. As I worked on this project, scurrying around to find money, making long canoe trips, I felt like I was on a mission from God. And being on a mission gave me tremendous energy.

The great Dr. Albert Schweitzer once said to a group of students, "I don't know what your destiny will be, but one thing I do know: the only ones among you who will be really happy are those who have sought and found how to serve."

Doing these projects fulfilled a lifelong dream of mine to directly help disadvantaged people. This, to me, is preferable to writing a check to a charity. There's nothing wrong with

81

writing a check to a charity, but I wanted more, and I got what I wanted.

As I said at the start of this chapter, I often wished for a book or mentor on how to do this work. I hope this chapter will help someone get started on this path.

I also hope that a few folks will see that having a mental illness is not a barrier to extraordinary accomplishment.

The world needs a lot of help. The way to do it is, don't get inundated by the scale of problems, just proceed one small step at a time.

CHAPTER 6

My Adventures As An Operative For The U.S. Government

Starting in 2005, I spent nine years doing counterintelligence work for the U.S. government.

I was an operative. As I wrote this chapter, I thought of using the word "spy" instead, but that feels a bit pretentious and show-offy to me. "Operative" is probably better. Technically speaking, I was a "confidential human source."

I didn't carry a gun. I didn't drive a silver Aston Martin with an ejector seat. But I did undercover work for a federal government agency. I don't want to identify the agency — I think it's better if I keep a few details under wraps.

Actually, I've got to tell you, I'm a little bit nervous writing at all about this part of my life. I seriously debated whether to include this chapter. But I'm including it because one of my goals here it to reduce the stigma of mental illness and inspire people to think, "Yeah, I can do that!"

It was exciting work, reasonably lucrative, and had elements of danger. It was perfect for me: As I've said in these pages, my bipolar disorder has enhanced my taste for adventure.

*

It all started in March of 2005 when I was working as a consultant for NASA arranging technology transfers to private industry. I was an expert in advanced materials including superalloys (heavy nickel-based materials for jet engines) and carbon composites (graphite fiber impregnated with resins; lightweight and strong).

One of my specialties was titanium, heavily used in defense industries. Titanium alloys have high tensile strength-to-density ratios and can withstand high temperatures. About two-thirds of global titanium is used in aircraft engines and frames; it's also used in naval vessels, missiles and spacecraft, and in many other areas, including medical implants, golf clubs and a 12-person all-titanium submarine for the U.S. Navy SEALs.

I attended a titanium trade show in Chicago in March of '05, sitting in NASA's booth and answering questions from people. I also gave a PowerPoint presentation to about 20 attendees.

Five days after I got home, I got a call from someone who identified himself as a NASA counterintelligence agent. I had no idea that NASA had such people on the payroll. This guy, Steve, wanted to meet with me. I said O.K.

A couple of days later I went to an office at NASA Glenn Research Center in Cleveland, known as NASA Glenn.

I met Steve in a room with concrete walls and no windows. It was probably a secure room, difficult or impossible to bug. Steve showed me his badge and credentials and introduced me to a guy named Jack, an agent for a national security organization.

Jack was interested in the Chicago trade show. He flipped on a tape recorder and asked me questions about it for more than an hour: What did I see, whom did I talk to.

He eventually informed me why his agency was so interested in the show: Someone from a major foreign power had approached people in the NASA booth (not me) and asked some delicate questions, basically inquiring if the NASA folks might be interested in doing a little bit of spying for this country (which I will refer to as "Nation X").

Jack and I wrapped things up. He turned off his tape recorder, put his papers away, looked at me closely and said:

"You know, Mike, you'd be an excellent person to work for us part-time."

"Work for you?"

"You're good on your feet. You can talk about a broad range of technologies. You own your own business so you have flexibility in your schedule. We need someone who can meet with business people and government officials and attend trade shows related to Nation X." He paused. "We would pay you for your time and expenses." He paused again. "Would you consider this?"

"Well…"

"I'm not saying anything definite will happen, but we have an immediate need for someone like you. And we're willing to pay."

I was immediately interested, even excited, but I maintained my cool, appropriate for a would-be operative: "Sure, I'll consider it."

"Can we begin a background check on you?"

"OK"

I told them right up front that I had bipolar disorder; they were fine with that. They accepted my assurance that I was managing my condition with good medications.

The security check took a couple of months. I made a little joke at one point. They had told me that the check was proceeding smoothly: "We haven't found any felonies on you." I said, "You haven't looked hard enough!" They were not amused. They looked at me and sort of squinted their eyes. I said, "Just a little joke there." Their expressions said, "This is no joke, dude." I said, "OK, no more jokes."

While the security clearance was going on, I met with Jack and his associates several times for lunch and instruction.

They told me about the interest of Nation X in various technologies. They gave me tips about what to expect at trade shows in Nation X. They told me what to do if I ever got into a bad spot overseas (call the embassy).

I passed the check (which included a polygraph test) and commenced my operative career in June 2005.

One aspect of my job, as I said, was to meet people at

trade shows and talk to them. I attended shows here in the U.S. and in Nation X. I also met people at Nation X's embassy in Washington and at its consulates.

My basic task was to develop relationships with people in order to gather information from them. Who works for what company. What a certain company specializes in. What are the relationships between companies. What technologies do people from Nation X talk about most.

I held hundreds of conversations with people from Nation X and reported what I learned to Jack and my other handlers. The fact that I was an independent consultant affiliated with NASA opened many doors for me.

Here's an example of how I did my job.

It's 2007. I'm attending a four-day titanium trade show at a big hotel in Boston. Fifteen hundred people have gathered in the hotel's ballroom (which is full of booths and tables) and in smaller side rooms. The show features schmoozing, gossiping, PowerPoint presentations, having a beer with people. My goal is to talk to every person I can from Nation X.

I'm my usual affable self. I build trust. I collect several dozen business cards. I hand out my card and discuss my consulting business. I keep an eye on what people are looking closely at and what they're photographing.

At this particular show there's a big cardboard cutout of a new U.S. Army weapons platform. The folks from Nation X are very interested in it; they take lots of photos, right out in the open. I make a mental note of that, and later include that tidbit in my report.

According to Jack, many people working for private companies in Nation X might be gathering information for their government. As I watch folks shoot photos of the weapons platform, I'm thinking, "They'll get brownie points when they're debriefed back home, and who knows, maybe they'll land nice government jobs as full-time spies."

I'm feeling pretty cool as I walk around this conference

floor, knowing that I'm the eyes and ears of the U.S. government in an area critical to national security. The twangy guitar theme from the James Bond films plays in my head.

Jack and I are hoping I'll get recruited at this show by Nation X to work for them. This would make me a double agent and open up a lot of new doors. (This didn't happen.)

On Day 2 of the show, I'm chatting with some folks at a table run by a titanium company from Nation X. We're all very friendly. I say, casually, "Oh, by the way, I have a friend who has a new process for making such-and-such an alloy, he's looking for investors." Ears prick up. They take my card. They're junior-level people; hopefully they'll give my card to some senior people and I'll be contacted. (This happens.)

I'm free to expand my consulting business while I'm here. Jack is entirely O.K. with that — in fact, he encourages it: "Go right ahead! Definitely! That'll be helpful for us!" At this particular show, I get hired by a guy, on the spot, as a consultant; he became a major client of mine for the next three years.

After the conference, I file a report with my agency. I make it a point to always file really good reports, above and beyond what they ask me to do, partly because that's the kind of worker I am, and partly for my own records and protection.

One time in 2007 I went to a party at a Nation X consulate here in the States. Jack had warned me that someone probably would come up to me at the party and try to get to know me really well. Sure enough, as I was standing there drinking wine and listening to music, an attractive young woman came up, said hello, and introduced herself. We chatted for 20 minutes. She was a citizen of Nation X pursuing an advanced degree from a major American college. I wasn't sure if she was the person Jack was talking about. I got her business card and said, "We're both here to network, do you want to continue talking after dinner?" She said yes but she left the party.

Jack was interested in this encounter and put her on a "watch list." Was she a spy? Trying to lure me into some sort of assignation? I don't know for sure, but it's entirely possible. Jack had me call her and take her out to dinner; she and I discussed an arrangement where she could represent my business in Nation X. I then suggested we meet with Nation X consulate officials to talk about our plans; she dropped me like a hot potato and I never heard from her again. To this day, I have no idea what was going on with her.

Having good people skills was a key for me in this work. It's a big reason I was hired in the first place. During my career as an operative, I made regular use of my empathy, creativity and interpersonal skills, which I believe are enhanced by my bipolar illness.

Whenever I told Jack about meeting someone interesting, he would ask me, "Would that person be good for us to contact in hopes of recruiting them for our side?" I gave him a few names, and offered my assessment of these people, but I never heard if anything happened.

At one point, about four years into my work, Jack said to me, "Your work is actually more fun than what we do." That made me feel pretty good.

At another point, Jack and I got to talking about the intelligence community and its structure. As we spoke, I realized that the community is set up just like an ordinary business, with a similar bureaucratic feel to it. In other words, it's not different from the real world, it's the same thing. Instead of manufacturing a product, they acquire intelligence.

*

I traveled to Nation X several times, visiting companies to talk about titanium and other advanced materials, and also discussing with them the possibility of my giving seminars about how technology transfer works. These were solid reasons for me to be there, talking to them, schmoozing, getting to know them.

The freakiest trip came in 2008 when I traveled to Nation X for a couple of conferences and meetings. Luanne came along as my executive assistant and note-taker, and also to help me assess people — she has great intuitive people skills. (She's also very classy and makes me look good.) And she came along because she wanted to protect me. She knew I was an operative. She worried about me, and wanted to be there for me, in case anything happened.

When you're working as an operative, isolated in a foreign country, any surprises will make you tense. On this trip, weird stuff happened.

When we checked in at our hotel, the credit card computer was supposedly "down."

I asked, "Do you know when it will be back up?"

"No, sir, we don't. Very sorry."

They wanted a cash deposit for us to stay there. I gave them what they wanted and they copied down all the serial numbers. This seemed weird to me. Was their demand for a huge deposit, and the copying, a stratagem for keeping tabs on me? Maybe.

We went to the conference the next morning. A strange man, who looked like a thug, kept taking pictures of me and of everyone with whom I spoke. This was weird.

We went back to our hotel room.

I'd been told by Jack that our room would probably be bugged. He also said that if I left a laptop computer there, it would probably be examined by Nation X operatives. He wanted me to leave an unattended laptop in the room; he hoped that the operatives would put a bug or virus in it, and that this bug could be examined by his agency.

I followed his instructions. I left my laptop in the room all that day.

Before I left the room that morning, I did a little bit of spycraft to monitor the situation. I plucked a hair from my head and put it in a little crevice in the computer. When we got back to the room later that day, sure enough, the hair had disappeared. Also, the computer wasn't working right. Nation X operatives had been in the room that day and gone through the machine. A few weeks later when we got home, Jack was very interested in what had happened and took my computer for examination.

*

The whole time we were there in '08, Luanne and I felt we were being followed or monitored. We picked up the weird vibe everywhere, on the street, in restaurants, sitting in the hotel lobby. We were fried with anxiety by the third day. We huddled under the sheets at night and whispered about whether we should pack up and leave.

Jack had told me that if I ever felt unsafe, I should go to the American embassy and ask for a legal attache, or "legat" (by which he meant a national security official). We went there on the fourth day. We had some trouble connecting with the right person on the embassy staff. I lost it. I blew up. I've lost my temper only about two times in my life and this was one of them. I shouted at one of the staff people, "MY SAFETY IS AT STAKE HERE. I NEED TO TALK TO SOMEONE NOW!!!"

It's amazing how fast people respond when someone is really yelling like that. We finally connected with a staff person who handed us a 35-page document that said, basically, "If you're working in a technology field, you should expect weird stuff to happen to you when you're visiting this country."

We calmed down a bit. I told Luanne, "Let's sleep on this and make a decision in the morning about staying or leaving."

We decided to stay.

The next day at the conference, the same strange man continued shooting pictures of me.

A couple of other strange things happened, and we continued to feel as if we were being watched, but we felt better prepared to deal with the weirdness, based on our knowledge of the 35-page document. I wish we had gotten that information before we started the trip.

*

The next week of our trip wasn't quite so traumatic; it was much more valuable in terms of gathering information and contacts.

We traveled to two other cities in Nation X. I attended meetings and also gave a PowerPoint presentation at a major technology transfer seminar about how NASA works with private industry. This included a detailed exposition about the solid lubricant PS300. Everything I said was a matter of public record, but the people in the audience may not have realized that.

I was quickly contacted by a person who I believe was part of their intelligence organization. He fit the profile; he was fluent in English, well-dressed, no business card, eager to talk about sensitive technologies. We had three meetings. I got the distinct impression that he wanted me to join their side.

In hindsight I wish I had said, "I have access to technology that isn't publicly available, perhaps we can work something out." But at the time, I wasn't willing to journey that far into the spy racket. I was aware that Americans had been arrested for low-level activity. For example, an American man photocopied publicly available data at a library in Nation X; when he got to the airport to go home, officials swooped down on him, busted him, and sent him to jail. As I said earlier, the idea of landing in a foreign prison is my worst nightmare.

Still, I gathered a lot of useful data on this trip, and Jack was extremely happy with my work.

*

In the wake of my work as an operative, I have a whole new level of admiration for people who do dangerous work for the U.S.A. in foreign countries. They're out there on the perimeter. They're risking their lives every day. They're protecting our interests and they're worthy of our greatest respect.

For me, the work was definitely stressful (but rewarding). The most stressful part was traveling in Nation X. Also stressful: working with the U.S. bureaucracy and not being told what happened as a result of my work.

*

I quit my operative career after nine years because the work started to peter out. The budget of the organization was cut, and I decided the work wasn't worth my time anymore.

My bipolar disorder was never once a negative factor in my work for the government. In fact, it probably helped, as I've indicated. I feel I'm living proof that some bipolar people, especially those of us who are on a good drug regimen, can handle anything.

I'm proud to have been an operative. Every big country has spies — Nation X probably has hundreds of spies in the U.S. — and we Americans need to do what we can to hold our own. I'm glad I was able to serve my country.

*

I had a funny little moment in 2006 with a psychiatrist who didn't believe that I was an operative.

I had been managing my bipolar disorder for many years, but occasionally I would feel clouds of sadness for a day or two or three. This happened in middle of May of '06.

My psychiatrist (we'll call her Dr. Morse) told me to slightly increase one of my medications and decrease the others. I mixed up instructions — I decreased one and increased the others. Big mistake. I went into a "mixed affective state":

agitated depression, with despair, suicidal thoughts and extreme irritability. It's a constant risk for bipolar people. Dr. Morse asked me if I needed to check into the psychiatric hospital, the same one where I had stayed in 1992.

I replied, "Yes."

Tears of anguish and hopelessness poured out of my eyes just as they had 14 years earlier. I felt something bad had taken over in me again, and I felt I'd never escape it.

It was a Friday evening. Luanne drove me to the hospital. Once again I walked down that long hallway.

The regular staff had gone home and the weekend people had signed on. I've got to say, the weekend staff didn't seem to know their jobs as well as the regular people.

I was asked a series of routine questions: what I did for a living, my drug history, how I was feeling. I described my career in detail, including my work as an operative. The admitting doctor frowned. He seemed kind of distracted. Then he nodded and said he would come by my room a little later.

My room was freezing cold. I tried to get an extra blanket but was told the cabinet was locked and they couldn't find the key. Great. I sat there shivering.

The admitting doctor came by an hour later and asked me how I was doing. I said, "I'm freezing!" He promised to get me some blankets. He said I should take a certain drug called Risperdal (the generic name is risperdone). It's an antipsychotic that I had never taken before. He was carrying a Risperdal tablet in a little vial and said, "Here you go."

I didn't trust this guy. I put my foot down: "I'll take my usual stuff but I'm not taking that! I'll ONLY take that if it's approved by my doctor." The admitting doctor said, "Mike, I would recommend you take it." I shouted, "NO WAY." So that was that.

Two hours later an attendant came by with a couple of thin cotton blankets. I was still cold. I was cold all night long.

My psychiatrist, Dr. Morse, corrected my meds on Saturday and told me it was O.K. to take Risperdal. I also changed rooms, got decent blankets and slept fine that night. I improved quickly, thank God.

On Monday morning, the head psychiatrist (we can call him Dr. O'Brian) talked to me for 20 minutes about my life: "What do you do for a living, Mike?"

I told him what I'd said to the admissions person on Friday: "I write music. I work for NASA. I have done humanitarian projects in the jungles of Borneo in Indonesia." I paused. "And in my spare time I work as an operative for a national security organization."

He looked a little bit confused, just like the other doctor. But he cleared me to leave; I checked out on Monday afternoon and went home.

A week later I saw Dr. Morse. She said, "Mike, Dr. O'Brian wanted to keep you there longer."

"Really?"

"He thinks you're delusional."

"Delusional?"

"He asked you about your career, right?"

"Yeah."

"And you told him about NASA? And the jungles of Borneo?"

"Yeah."

"And being an operative?"

I paused. I was getting the picture.

Dr. Morse said, "Mike, Dr. O'Brian's diagnosis was 'clearly delusional.'"

"But I told the truth about myself!"

"I know that. You know that. But Dr. O'Brian wanted to keep you in the hospital for observation."

We laughed at the absurdity of the situation.

"If you go to an emergency room for a broken arm," Dr. Morse continued, "they always ask you what you do for a living. If you tell them about being an operative and so forth, they'll think you're psychotic, and they won't discharge you until you talk to a psychiatrist. Maybe the psychiatrist won't show up for a while — six hours, eight hours. Maybe not until the next morning or Monday morning. You'll be stuck there. And if you just walk out, your insurance won't pay your emergency room bill, because you weren't formally discharged."

In other words, this was your basic Catch-22 situation, where you can't win either way. I've always remembered her advice. She was my doctor for the next five years; every now and then she'd say, "Don't tell people what you do!" I'm prepared to prevaricate if I ever get in a tough spot.

"Don't tell people what you do!" — the greatest compliment I ever got

CHAPTER 7

My Adventures As A Mental Health Volunteer

I walked into Lutheran Hospital in Cleveland in July 2013 and took the elevator to the psychiatric ward on the third floor. I was there to speak with a dozen or so people suffering from mental illnesses: depression, bipolar disorder, schizophrenia and so on.

I was a new volunteer for the National Alliance on Mental Illness, known as NAMI (pronounced "nah-mee"). My talk would have two parts: a detailed description of my struggle with bipolar disorder, and a review of the help available to these folks when they got out of the hospital in a few days or weeks, including NAMI support groups and educational courses.

As I walked into the ward, I reminded myself of my basic guidelines: I can't make people feel better about themselves, nor can I tell folks what to do, but I can share my road to recovery, and I can let them know they're not alone. Those messages carry hope. Social isolation is bad news; networks are good news.

*

I started thinking about volunteering in early 2013 when my friend Art told me he gave free trumpet lessons to disadvantaged kids. His eyes glowed as he told me how much fun he was having. I thought, "I need to be doing something like this! Otherwise I'm just a selfish schmuck!" I began casting around for a volunteer gig.

Actually, I was already a volunteer. I had done the

project in Borneo. I knew that volunteering could be deeply rewarding. What new activity would grab me with the same intensity as my adventure in Indonesia? I wanted something that would be fun, challenging and genuinely useful to society. I have a special tactic when I'm faced with a big life decision or I'm looking for a solution to a problem: I ask my subconscious mind for help. I asked myself, "What type of volunteer should I be? Music? Something else?" Then I stop actively thinking about the question and let my deep brain poke around for an answer. I know that my subconscious will come forth with something because this tool has always worked for me.

I needed two weeks to find my answer. One morning I suddenly said to myself:

"I know a lot about being bipolar. I endured 30 years with no treatment and I've had 21 years of successful recovery and management of my illness. I can share what I know and help people."

Perfect!

Art told me about an organization called Greater Cleveland Volunteers where I could get guidance on how to take this idea and turn it into an action plan. I called them up and said, "I'm a world-class expert on being bipolar; is there anyone who could benefit from my experience?" The woman with whom I spoke said, "Let me check." She called me back 10 minutes later and said "Mike, the National Alliance on Mental Illness, NAMI, is an excellent option for you."

I had never heard of NAMI. I did some research. I liked their websites (nami.org[5] and namigreatercleveland.org[6]) and decided to pay a visit at the office of NAMI Greater Cleveland on 25th Street downtown.

*

NAMI was founded in the late 1970s. It's a nonprofit. It's America's largest grassroots mental health organization; it has offices in many cities. It offers support groups for people with mental illnesses and their families. It publishes a magazine, advocates with lawmakers, explains treatment options, raises money through walk-athons and other efforts, teaches job skills, fights stigma in the media, trains people on computers, offers a variety of classes, and operates a help line for anyone who needs advice on a severe mental illness (1-800-950-NAMI; the number of the Cleveland office is 216-875-7776).

NAMI covers the waterfront, offering information at its website about ADHD, anxiety disorders, autism, bipolar disorder, borderline personality disorder, depression, dissociative disorders, eating disorders, obsessive-compulsive disorder, post-traumatic stress disorder, schizoaffective disorder and schizophrenia. Also: anosognosia, dual diagnosis, psychosis, self-harm, sleep disorders and suicide.

NAMI also sends volunteers to hospitals with information packets and answers to questions.

Volunteers, in my opinion, are essential to the American social fabric. Volunteerism provides a lot of the glue that holds together our chaotic nation — people who spend a few hours a week or more working for NAMI, the Girl Scouts and Boy Scouts, fire departments, political parties, schools, libraries, literacy programs, food banks, meals on wheels, soup kitchens, film festivals, chess clubs, adopt-a-highway programs, crisis hotlines, hospices, children's advocacy groups, animal shelters, Big Brothers and Big Sisters and athletic teams. Just to name a few.

Moreover, volunteering can help people learn new skills, be a part of their community, gain a sense of achievement, improve their career prospects, and meet and inspire new people. And I would add this: volunteering makes me feel grateful for what I have and thankful I'm able to give to others.

Dr. Joseph Mercola wrote in 2013:

> Volunteering is a simple way to help others, but it's also a powerful way to help yourself. ... New research from Carnegie Mellon University followed more than 1,000 adults between the ages of 51 and 91. Those who volunteered for at least 200 hours a year were 40 percent less likely to develop high blood pressure than those who did not. The type of volunteer work appeared to be irrelevant. Rather, it was the amount of time spent doing it that mattered. Social interaction, and the stress relief it can provide, is likely one major reason why volunteering has a beneficial effect on blood pressure; it's a well-known fact that stress elevates blood pressure. Volunteering is not only a boon for your heart health. Research shows volunteering can cut your overall mortality risk by 47 percent, and may lower your risk of depression and anxiety, and boost your psychological well-being. The benefits are particularly pronounced among older adults.

*

I liked the vibe of the NAMI Greater Cleveland office. The staff members were friendly and welcoming and seemed very much on the ball. (A few months after my initial visit, NAMI Greater Cleveland won a national NAMI award for "Outstanding Affiliate of 2014.")

Jennifer, the volunteer coordinator, explained my options. If I wanted to keep things low key and low pressure, I could do office work, such as photocopying and filing. I said I wanted something that would require serious effort. Jennifer smiled and steered me to their Speakers Bureau, where volunteers are trained to visit hospitals and connect with the patients (who are referred to as "peers").

Barbara, manager of the bureau, told me that the hospital visitation program of NAMI Greater Cleveland is one of the most active such efforts in the country. Volunteers in northeastern Ohio make many dozens of hospital visits monthly and serve thousands of people.

She and I talked for a while. She said, "I think you'll be very good at this." She invited me to sign up, which I did.

I went through formal training spread over four Saturdays. NAMI did a legal background check on me.

After my training, I went through an apprenticeship, accompanying Jennifer on about 10 hospital visits to see how she did it.

During these weeks, I pondered the fact that no outreach program had existed when I was in the psychiatric hospital in 1992. NAMI wasn't up and running yet at the place where I stayed. I could have used the additional help.

In July of '13 I was fully trained and ready to go.

I wasn't nervous as I walked into Lutheran Hospital that morning. I like getting up in front of people and talking. I've always felt totally comfortable as a speaker and presenter. Maybe my years of musical performing, and the many presentations I've given in my business career, are partly responsible for my confidence in front of an audience. After I publish this book, I'm looking forward to sharing my experiences with larger audiences.

*

I was buzzed into the psychiatric unit through locked doors. (Ah! Locked doors again! But I didn't freak out.) I walked past two security guards (they were very friendly and welcoming) and entered a common room/TV room where 11 people were seated at a long cafeteria table. It was a reasonably cheerful setting, with sunlight streaming in from narrow windows.

The guards kept an eye on things through windows facing the hallway.

I met my NAMI co-presenter, Hannah, with whom I had spoken on the phone a few days earlier. She was very pleasant.

In the group of 11 peers, several people smiled and had expressions of curiosity and interest; several seemed distracted; several looked like they would rather be anyplace else.

I could tell that two of the people were bipolar. Something in their eyes, manner, and talkativeness — the confident persona they put out. I always feel like I'm a sort of cousin of other people with bipolar disorder because there's something in our personalities that is the same. I feel as if we are in some sort of bipolar club.

Hannah and I sat down and the meeting commenced. We got right to the point. I said, "We're from the National Association on Mental Illness, NAMI. My name is Mike. I'm diagnosed with bipolar Type I."

"My name is Hannah," said my partner. "I have schizophrenia."

This broke the ice. Most of the 11 people now looked attentive.

We went around the table and asked people for their first names. We explained that we never use last names, we never ask about diagnoses, and we never discuss specific medications.

I spent 15 minutes telling them the basic version of my life story: my depressive episodes starting when I was a teenager, how I didn't get a diagnosis until I reached my mid-20s, my denial of being bipolar even after the diagnosis, my attempts to self-medicate, my plan to kill myself, my hospitalization at age 39.

I could tell that I was connecting with most of my audience.

I told them about many of the things I did after I finally got my medications figured out: Borneo, consulting for NASA, writing songs.

They loved that.

I said, "I have a right to be depressed. It's OK for me to be who I am. I don't owe an explanation to anybody."

They really loved that.

Hannah then told her story for 15 minutes. She started hearing voices when she was a teenager. Her mother thought she was using illegal drugs. She couldn't get the help she needed for a long time but finally ended up in a mental health ward for three months. She took an experimental medication and did well on it, but she couldn't stay on it because it wasn't approved yet by the FDA for wide use. She went home, but pretty soon needed to go back to the hospital, again for three months. The second time around, they found the right medicines for her.

She related how people actually argue with her about whether she's schizophrenic or not because she looks and acts so "normal."

People nodded as she spoke. One woman seemed ready to cry. They could tell that Hannah had walked the walk.

NAMI has a bounty of programs and courses, including support groups facilitated by trained peers where people tell their stories and connect emotionally (a lot of group wisdom gets shared in these), art therapy, music, journaling, faith-based support groups, and poetry-based groups. We also mentioned other organizations that could provide assistance.

Most of the peers listened carefully. One guy raised his hand and asked whether NAMI would help him find post-hospital housing.

"No, we don't," Hannah said, "but the hospital staff can work with you to find a group home or other housing."

I added, "We have more information on the handout we'll give you, including phone numbers of agencies that will help you find housing."

A woman asked if NAMI charged anything for making use of its resources. I had mentioned earlier that everything was free; I repeated that.

A young woman raised her hand shyly and said quietly,

"My father says I shouldn't take my medicines. He says they're evil." She spoke for a few minutes about her difficult home situation. We answered by telling about our experiences with medications and how much they had helped us, and mentioned that she should bring this up with her doctors and/ or caseworker.

A woman in her early 20s asked if she could join my family and come to live with us. I felt very sorry for her, that she didn't have a good family environment, but I'd been trained to not try to answer impossible questions like that. I moved on, gently.

The peers asked a number of additional questions, which we answered. We then handed out blue two-pocket folders with brochures and phone numbers. We also gave out evaluation sheets for the peers to rate our presentation. (NAMI keeps very good statistics to show to prospective funders.) And that was that. About an hour all told.

Several of the peers came up to us afterward and thanked us. Nurses and other staff people thanked us effusively as we left. Staff folks are almost invariably really fine people.

"I feel drained," I said to Hannah. She nodded and said, "Me too."

At the same time, I felt satisfied with our session. (In fact, I almost always feel satisfied with sessions.) Several of the people at the meeting really absorbed our message — I could see this on their faces. They came to a new place of hope. They realized they could lead happy and productive lives. They saw they could make it if they took their meds, saw their doctor and therapist, and took advantage of resources such as support groups.

*

I've continued giving presentations ever since, averaging nine a month. My fellow volunteers have been consistently great to work with — Hannah and many others.

I've had a few interesting adventures. Nothing hugely dramatic. I've encountered two or three very tough-looking customers in my groups who have come up to me afterward and said, "When did you get out?" "Out of where?" "Prison." "Uhhh … I've never been in prison." "Oh. OK Never mind. You didn't miss anything."

One time a guy sat across the table from me. He was 6-foot-2 and solid muscle. He said, "I was involved in a crime. I got shot five times. I went to prison." He paused. He continued, "I'm here on the insanity plea." (He was very proud of that.) I nodded, as calmly as I could. He could have beaten me up with one hand tied behind his back. This was the one time I felt nervous, out of the thousands of people I've seen and spoken to. We had been instructed on how to deal with situations like that: stay calm, exit if you feel you need to, etc.

On several occasions, security guards have stood near certain patients, maybe two or three feet behind them. I never found out why this protocol was followed, but I felt glad the guards were there.

Patients sometimes look out for our well-being by warning us about a person's potential behavior or confronting someone who keeps interrupting. On one occasion, a woman in a wheelchair sat behind me. I was cautioned by another woman: "You need to watch her. She might stab you."

"Stab me with what?"

"A plastic fork. She stabbed me with a plastic fork at breakfast." I kept an eye out for trouble and emerged unstabbed.

Another time, a woman came up to me in the hallway and said, "I'm a piano player and composer. They transported my brain back through time; I wrote music for Beethoven and Bach."

I didn't laugh. I'm certainly not laughing now. I look upon her as a person in trouble (just as I was once) who deserves the best care possible and hopefully can find solace, sanctuary and healing.

One time, a young guy interrupted a few times with questions:

"Did you run over any aluminum foil on your way to the hospital?" "Can I buy NAMI for twenty dollars?" "Do you eat pancakes at 2 a.m.?" My nature is to be nice to everybody and let people talk if they want to. If someone is interrupting a lot, to where it's interfering with the flow of the meeting, he or she needs to be told to pipe down. This is difficult for me. I ask other volunteers to kick me in the leg if someone is too disruptive and I'm not realizing it.

I would estimate that I get stressed-out at about half of these meetings, with people interrupting, not listening, coming and going. I'm OK with that level of stress. I've learned techniques for managing the stress, including remembering to breathe, smiling, relaxing my shoulders — and, if necessary, getting a staff person to remove a troublemaker.

Another thing I've learned is the value of putting on a good show. Before my presentation, when I'm in my car, I shout, "It's showtime!" like Roy Scheider in *All That Jazz*, to get the adrenaline flowing. I try to bring some of that Broadway stage energy to my group. I inject humor and keep things bright and upbeat.

One time, when I gave a presentation at a local hospital, it was total chaos. No staff people were on hand to provide me with support. People wandered in and out. The meeting started with four peers; others came and left. I handed out 12 folders. The meeting ended with three peers. One peer couldn't read. Another stared into space. I couldn't keep control and got really stressed out. Afterward, I thought briefly about quitting as a volunteer. But I didn't. I got right back up on the horse, kept at it, and got better at maintaining control.

I complained about my chaotic experience to a fellow volunteer, my friend Peter. He mentioned his worst day as a volunteer. This had happened two weeks earlier. Peter was standing at a nurse's station near a guy who was being discharged. Peter walked away from the station for a few moments, and suddenly there was a lot of noise. The patient who had just been discharged had walked out to a parking area and jumped four floors to his death. He lay in a crumpled heap on the concrete.

Peter cried. Everyone on the floor cried.

Health is so fragile. A life can end in an instant.

Every life is precious. Every life deserves support and love. This is tough work sometimes. Some people try to do this work and can't take it; they freak out.

*

As of this writing, I've made more than 400 volunteer visits for NAMI. I've spoken to some 3,000 people at three institutions in the Cleveland area: Lutheran and Marymount Hospitals and Highland Springs, a behavioral hospital. (I've also done a few visits at other hospitals.) I am also a substitute peer support group leader.

I was tremendously honored in 2017 to be given the Scott Adamson Memorial Peer Award from NAMI Greater Cleveland. I was given a beautiful glass sculpture at a big banquet; I keep this on my desk. (Scott Adamson was an active member of NAMI Greater Cleveland who died in 2009.)

I feel honored that I'm allowed to do this work. I feel good about making a concrete contribution to the mental health of my community. I hope to continue volunteering for NAMI for years to come.

CHAPTER 8

My Adventures With Creativity

I hate my bipolar disorder.
And I thank God that I'm bipolar.
I occasionally get down on my knees before climbing into bed and thank the Lord for four things: being alive, having a wonderful marriage, having the ability to contribute something positive to the world, and having bipolar disorder.

The main reason I hate being bipolar is, it's a serious illness.

The main reason I thank God for my illness is that it has enhanced my creativity.

Creativity is central to who I am; it's a foundation of my soul, my karma, my chi, my life force, my vibe. It informs so much of what I do; maybe it informs everything I do.

I love thinking in offbeat ways about problems and finding solutions. I love saying "What if?" I love that moment when a fresh and useful thought pops into my head after days or weeks of pondering. I love carving my own path.

Being creative has made my life much more interesting than it might otherwise have been. So the connections are: Bipolar = Enhanced Creativity = a Better Life.

Some bipolar people worry that being on medications will damage their creativity. I don't find this to be true for me. I perhaps create less stuff (music, etc.) today, but the work that comes out is just as good as ever.

I sometimes feel like I want to climb up on a rooftop and shout to the world "Bipolar disorder is great!"

I know that sounds — ahem — crazy.

Maybe this book is the equivalent of a rooftop shout.

*

Now, I want to quickly add, many bipolar people, especially those who haven't been treated effectively, are in serious pain. I myself have been through a fair bit of pain, as I've shown in this book. Perhaps I should modify my exuberance a little bit. For me, today, bipolar disorder is great, because (a) My drug regimen is carefully designed, well-monitored and effective; (b) I take really good care of myself; (c) I have strong support from family and friends; (d) The illness helps me be creative; and (e) I've decided to focus on the positives of the disorder rather than the negatives, most prominently creativity, but also empathy, the ability to connect with others.

*

I believe virtually all human beings are creative. I naturally include virtually all bipolar people in that statement. Not everyone can write *War and Peace* or "Like a Rolling Stone," but everyone is creative to some extent. (If you don't believe me, stop by any kindergarten and check out the buzz of activity. As Picasso said, "Every child is an artist.")

I believe that all bipolar people owe it to themselves to fully explore their creativity, to embrace it, to celebrate it on a daily basis.

Ditto for all human beings!

*

Journalist and consultant Jon Rappoport has helped a number of clients over the years unleash their personal creativity. He writes:

Life wants to create. Creating is, to the spirit, what breathingis to the body.

Every person has his/her own take on reality. Every person on the planet is different. Systems and organizations don't recognize that. It is that personal point of view which gives birth to creative solutions. When I use the term "creative solutions," I mean solutions to life itself. Spirit and soul are restless. Because they want to create something new, something large. They want to launch.

The culture of a society takes pride in defining boundaries and limits. That's the way of civilization. So be it. But the individual is different. At some level of his consciousness, he is looking for a way out, because he knows his ambitions are primarily aimed at something "wider and higher and deeper."

*

Here's a quote that I came across on the Internet: "Unhappiness is an accident; productivity, creativity, and pleasure are the metaphysical essentials of life."

*

As a kid, I never once said, "I'm creative." Nor did I think it or imagine it. I would have been called a braggart if I had played around with that idea, and being a braggart was bad news.

I learned as an adult that lots of kids are encouraged from the cradle to be creative, and this fact actually surprised me a little bit. These lucky kids have great teachers; maybe they go to a Montessori school and are given blocks of time to pursue their interests; maybe their parents are artists (or frustrated artists). These kids go deeply and passionately into music or sculpture or drawing or theater or building models or computer coding; they spend hours engaged in a creative task; they become accustomed to thinking of themselves as creative – and lo and behold, they ARE creative.

If I had gotten a better start in music, or in painting or writing, I might have gone down a different path in life. (I hope I'm not being whiny about this — my real point here is to say to parents, "Help your kids, gently!")

My parents never said a word to me about creativity even though my father was a professional musician. He didn't see himself as being particularly creative. He never wrote music even though he had a wealth of knowledge about music theory and composition that he had learned from three years of study at the Cleveland Institute of Music. He saw himself as a working guy trying to make a living in a tough business.

My teachers didn't place much emphasis on creativity. Their idea of instruction was to get their students to memorize and recite a lot of facts. Catholic grade schools in Cleveland devoted little to no classroom time to art.

I started piano lessons when I was 10. This was basically a disaster. My teacher, let's call her Mrs. Knight, had no sense of fun or adventure, no feel for the romance of the piano, and total hatred for rock 'n' roll piano. I sat there playing scales and etudes from the Diller-Quaile workbook, with Mrs. Knight nodding in a bored sort of way. I quit after a year. I continued with the trumpet, but part of my musical creativity had been stifled.

A year later, a teacher told my parents that I had some definite talent for drawing and painting, and suggested that I take classes at the Cleveland Institute of Art, which I did for the summer. So, yeah, there's an example of my parents helping me, but it turned out badly.

I had the worst teacher in the history of art instruction. Let's call him Mr. Quinn. He was a sad, schlumpy guy with very

113

little energy. He hardly said a word to me; I was the youngest kid in the class and apparently wasn't worth his attention. After every session, Mr. Quinn took each student's work and taped it to the blackboard ranked "best" to "worst" (in his opinion). My stuff was almost always rated "worst" (one time, I was second worst). I'll never forget looking up at my work on that board, looking at my peers, and saying, "I can't do it. I'm a failure. I'm not creative."

I shut down a big chunk of my creative self.

But not all of it.

I mentioned earlier in the book that when I was 16 I organized a 200-mile canoe trip in Ohio for myself and two friends, Steve and Chris. We started on the Mohican River and progressed to other rivers: the Black Fork, the Walhonding, the Muskingum.

None of us had ever canoed before. The only camping we'd done was in our backyards. These facts did not faze me. I just thought it up and did it, and it was one of the most fun experiences of my life.

I realize now this was a creative venture. I didn't think of it that way at the time. The word I put on it was "fun." If I had also used the word "creative" — if I had been O.K. with thinking, "I'm creative, and this is fun!" — I might have fanned some of my creativity flames. Language has a lot of power! Just repeating the phrase "I am creative!" has power!

During my teens, I played the trumpet and started up again on the piano (no lessons, just for my own enjoyment). Piano has certain advantages for anyone interested in music. It has the four elements of music where trumpet only has two. In other words, piano has melody, harmony, rhythm, and timbre, or tone, while the trumpet has just melody and tone. As I mentioned earlier, I played trumpet with several groups: the high school concert band and jazz band, Case Western Reserve's concert band, and a Motown-influenced band. I played for a touring production of *Man of La Mancha*. And I played with a band that supported Lou Rawls on a three-concert tour of Ohio.

This was creative stuff, no question about it, but as noted, I didn't think of myself that way and didn't let the phrase "I am creative" fully inform my life. I let it inform just a sliver of my life, a modest little percentage.

*

Another example of creativity was how I got myself into college. When I was 14, my father told me I'd have to pay for college myself because he and my mom couldn't afford it. I said "OK" and put together a plan. I had no one to guide me. No one in my family had ever gone to college. My high school counselors didn't seem interested in me.

I made college happen.

I think, maybe, that during those years a little voice deep inside me was saying, "Expand your life." That voice was my creativity talking. Sometimes the voice is hard to hear, but it's always present, in pretty much everyone.

*

I would like to comment on the relationship between creativity and risk.

For me, they're tied together in some interesting ways. They both offer new feel-good stimuli. They both pump me up.

I mentioned the canoe trip I took when I was 16. That was creative, and risky, so it hit a sweet spot for me.

When I was a sophomore in college I went on a five-day winter backpacking trip in the Allegheny National Forest in Pennsylvania. I had never done a winter backpacking trip before. Creative, risky … perfect.

I've done tons of backpacking and sailing. For me these activities offer exactly the right combination of (a) creativity; (b) risk, difficulty, challenge; and (c) peace of mind. The day we hike out of the woods, to go home, I say to my friend Steve,

"Throw me another week of food and I'll keep going. I don't want to go back." Steve laughs, and of course we go home.

My Borneo adventures combined creativity and risk.

All that said, I think it's entirely possible to be creative without risk. For example, someone might like to paint flowers. No risk there at all, but plenty of creativity. Not my cup of tea, but for some people, an absolutely wonderful way to get the creative juices flowing. And getting those juices flowing is important for happiness, whether risk is involved or not.

*

When I was young, I would tell people, "I don't know what I want to be when I grow up." I was under the impression that I would be limited to doing just one thing as an adult.

I realized in my 40s that I didn't need to do one thing, I could do lots of things.

Work was part of it. Composing and playing music was part of it. The Borneo project was part of it.

I finally understood that I could apply my creativity to all of these areas. I could lead a truly creative life.

*

Writing a piece of music is what I call "intimate" creativity. I love sitting at my keyboard for hours experimenting with melody, rhythm and the other elements of composition. I'm looking forward to posting some of my music on YouTube.

Creativity can be more than music and art, of course. What I call "problem-solving" creativity can contribute to the development of new products and technologies.

My career as a problem solver blossomed in the 1980s at the Clevite Corporation, a former manufacturing company based in Cleveland. It was a significant U.S. defense contractor involved with batteries, fuel cells, transistors, titanium powder, torpedoes for submarines, copper foil, automotive components

116

and many other products. I was a business development manager working in R&D, evaluating new inventions for business opportunities, interviewing engineers and business people, contacting potential customers and joint venture partners. I was also involved with a technology that bonded engineering polymers to metal.

This was heaven for me. I loved how the job allowed me to be creative in a constantly changing environment (and to make good money). Unfortunately, the R&D division was shut down in 1990.

I then started my own consulting company specializing in advanced materials. This was an important decision for me because it represented freedom. I enjoyed freelancing: I had tons of flexibility and a lot of room for creativity. It kept me on my toes every day and made me work fast and smart. I always knew I could walk out the door if the work environment or client became stultifying or stupid.

In 1999, while still running my own firm, I was hired as a consultant by Battelle, the world's largest nonprofit R&D organization. They were a subcontractor for NASA; my job was to work for NASA Glenn Reseach Center. When NASA scientists invented something, I would study the new technology, talk with people about its implications, and think of ways to get it out into the world. One of our goals was to create jobs. Another was to improve American productivity.

For example, NASA developed an awesome solid lubricant called PS300 as a critical component in a nuclear reactor system powering the Cassini-Huygens mission to Saturn. PS300 is stable at high temperatures and is adaptable to many different conditions. I found uses for it in the electricity industry for lubrication of steam turbines. One energy company that adopted PS300 saved millions of dollars in operating costs by putting the coating on stainless steel valves. PS300 has also been used in advanced aeropropulsion engines and refrigeration.

One time at NASA Glenn, I was assigned to find more commercial applications for their wind tunnels. As my team planned this work, I mentioned that we should do benchmarking in a certain way that would gain us a lot of competitive information without undue effort. No one else had ever heard of this type of benchmarking. My idea got the green light, I did the work, and we obtained a tremendous amount of information about our competitors. My contribution dwarfed anyone else's. Our project was a big success.

My supervisor at NASA Glenn was a very bright woman named Pierette Woodford. I asked her to write a comment for this book. Here's her response:

> Our responsibility was to transfer technologies from NASA and other federal laboratories to industry with a particular emphasis on small enterprises. These transfers can be quite complicated and involve a lot of creative thinking to tweak the technologies for their new applications and understand how to work through the many issues of intellectual property. Mike seemed to be just the person we were looking for. His curiosity about technology, his non-linear thinking, and his work ethic quickly became a great addition to our team. Mike stimulated us in looking for unusual approaches and solutions. His creativity was contagious. When I needed to refresh my energy I often would walk into his office for a smile and another way to look at what was going on with our team of engineers and business experts. Mike never failed us!

I'm pretty proud of that statement. She also said to me (years ago), "Mike, I like the way you think. You think differently from everyone else here."

Thanks, Pierette!

While I'm at it, I'd like to include another testimonial. This is from another guy I worked for during the '90s:

> As an outside consultant, Mike worked on several Fortune 500 projects while I was president and owner of Gorham Advanced Materials Institute. These projects were in the areas of technology assessment, strategic business planning, market research, and business valuation. Our projects were fast-paced and required real-time changes in direction as new information was acquired. In addition, there was no prescribed roadmap on how to carry out the project. We needed a high level of problem-solving and analysis of data on a daily basis. Mike's creative inputs proved valuable. His sense of humor and affability were essential to maintaining smooth working relationships among team members and clients.

I also want to include here a short description of my consulting company, which is still active, creative and thriving.

Trzcinski & Company LLC
Michael Trzcinski, president of Trzcinski & Company, helps businesses and governmental organizations in the decision-making process required for investments, joint ventures and licenses related to new products and technology. Our clients need the best information from outside their companies, and to develop relationships with new companies. Pursuing these requirements often involves interviews, discussion or negotiations with leading technical experts and business management.

Since 1990, Trzcinski & Company has realized a number of competitive advantages and cost-effective processes by:

- applying extensive industry knowledge and experience

- utilizing a proprietary international contact database

- sustaining personal relationships in the industries served

- developing alliances with other consulting organizations

- employing well-developed interviewing and negotiation skills.

- When it becomes difficult or costly for an organization to obtain information, develop relationships or maintain anonymity when conducting research, Trzcinski & Company provides expertise and services.

*

I think creativity is hard-wired into us as a source of satisfaction.

People talk about the value of eating "paleo" — eating like our Paleolithic ancestors supposedly ate many thousands of years ago and reconnecting with our roots. (The Paleolithic period lasted from roughly 2.6 million years ago to about 10,000 years ago.) I believe that our Paleolithic forebears led intensely creative lives and that this contributed as much to their health and vigor as their diet. They studied and interpreted the signs of nature: the behavior of animals, the bounty of plants, the movements of the sun, the ebb and flow of the sea and of rivers. They pondered the mysteries of the night sky and told stories about it. They decided where to trek. They solved daily challenges of finding food. They invented language, devised tools, and developed religions and spirituality.

They gave birth to art. There is no more beautiful and deeply felt art in the history of humanity than the cave and rock paintings of various cultures.

*

In the 1970s, academic researchers began studying the relationships between psychiatric disorders and creativity. (Poets and philosophers have speculated about this topic for centuries, of course.)

Dr. Nancy Andreasen of the University of Iowa was a pioneering researcher in this realm. In one of her studies, she surveyed a large group of prominent authors and found that 80 percent had experienced at least one episode in their lives of a major mood disorder; this compared with 30 percent in a control group. Andreasen followed these authors through the 1980s and learned that 43 percent had bipolar disorder, compared with only 10 percent of the control group.

To me, those numbers are pretty darn convincing that there's something interesting going on here.

(By the way, here is Andreasen's list of personality traits that define creative people: openness to experience, adventurousness, rebelliousness, sensitivity, playfulness, persistence, curiosity. I would add that creative people don't see the world in black and white and are comfortable in the gray areas.)

Academic research continued through the '90s and into the '00s. In 2007, Claudia M. Santosa and her team at Stanford University published a study in The Journal of Affective Disorders offering a wealth of new data. She and her team used a measure of creativity called the Barron-Welsh Art Scale, where participants draw images that are then analyzed. Santosa found that people with bipolar disorder scored significantly higher for creativity than a non-bipolar control group. Santosa summarized: "After three decades of research, there is persuasive, if not definitive, evidence linking creativity with bipolar disorders."

The next question is, why this link? I want to offer a provocative quote from Dr. Neel Burton, a British psychiatrist and author:

> Genes for potentially debilitating disorders such as bipolar disorder usually pass out of the population over time because affected people have fewer children. The fact that this has not happened for bipolar disorder suggests that the responsible genes are being maintained despite their potentially debilitating effects on a significant proportion of the population, and thus that they must be conferring an important adaptive or evolutionary advantage.

Maybe God, or Mother Nature, is saying, "Let's keep those bipolar genes working; they're good for humanity."

I have a personal theory about the link between creativity and bipolar disorder.

The human brain continues to develop as a person reaches his 20s. My disorder first manifested itself when I was a teenager. With those two facts as background, I make this statement: I believe my disorder affected the development of my brain by creating nerve synapses that supported creativity — in other words, my illness directly influenced my bent toward creativity.

Among the characteristics of the manic cycle of bipolar disorder are very fast, or racing, thoughts and amped-up energy — superhighways, let's say, of ideas, creating new ideas, creating more new ideas. My disorder generated a superhighway of creative energy when I was 16, 17, 18 years old, a crucial time for brain development. Lots of fresh synapses in my head! My brain became wired in a way that supports creativity!

Meanwhile, because of the pain and trauma of this period, the depressive cycle of bipolar disorder, I developed an inclination toward empathy.

In short, I believe that my illness directly laid the groundwork for my creativity and empathy. This idea has not been studied by scientists, to the best of my knowledge. I wonder if there's a way for scientists to dig into my theory?

*

I always mention creativity when I'm speaking to hospital groups as a volunteer for NAMI, the National Alliance on Mental Illness. Among my comments:

"Creativity feels good."

"You may need a nudge to help you realize you're creative. So take a class! If you end up with a bad teacher, bag that class, take another one!"

"YouTube has thousands of video lessons for everything under the sun. It's a great way to learn because it's visual and because you can start and stop the lesson as needed. Just the other day I punched 'pottery lessons for beginner' into YouTube and got dozens of choices. (Of course, now the question is, which ones do I choose?)"

"Digital technology is a godsend for creativity. You owe it to yourself to get familiar with what computers and digital gear can do. You can have a supercomputer on your desk for $1,500 and a perfectly good computer for less than $400. (And you can use the computer free at your local library.) Meanwhile, digital cameras have made photography far cheaper than what it cost in the era of film and darkrooms. And you might want to wander through your local Guitar Center and get a feel for the incredible possibilities of digital music."

"Have you ever participated in a drum circle? A poetry reading? An open mic at a comedy club? Have you ever checked out what your library offers in the way of free classes? Have you ever checked out the catalog of your local community college?"

"Read *Drawing on the Right Side of the Brain* by Betty Edwards. Even if you don't end up drawing, you're going to learn a lot from her about creativity, how it's encouraged, how it gets choked off."

"Sometimes, involvement precedes interest; getting involved in something can help you develop an interest in it."

"If you're over 50 and looking around for something creative to do, join AARP. They have comprehensive resources."

"Doing something creative can feel scary. Remember: In any creative activity, getting started is half the battle."

"All of my major accomplishments are a result of the creativity and empathy that sprang from my disorder."

*

My medications have evened me out. The highs aren't as high; the lows aren't as low. This is a good thing. I'm saner and happier. And, as I mentioned, my creativity is still at a very high level.

I'm somewhat less interested in big adventures than when I was young but I still like a certain amount of risk. I'm planning voyages on my newly purchased sailboat, a 30-footer. I'm planning a backpacking trip to New Zealand in Arthur's Pass National Park, which has some extremely challenging terrain.

One of my goals is to move my risk-taking to a deeper, richer place. For example, I'm working up the courage to write a piece of music that tells about my experience in the psychiatric hospital. I'm thrilled by that idea and kind of scared too.

Writing music is a wonderful way to get my feelings out. As I contemplate this new musical project, I tell myself, "Risk is good." I then tell myself, "I'm a creative person." I see the connection between those two things. And I tell myself, "Go for it!"

Above all, I don't want to be sitting in a rocking chair in my 90s saying "I should have done that."

CHAPTER 9

Frequently Asked Questions About Bipolar Disorder

Q. Is there a website that offers good, solid, readable, up-to-date information about bipolar disorder?

A. Yes. It's nimh.nih.gov, the website of the National Institute of Mental Health[7] (NIMH).

Q. What advice would you give to someone who is worried about being bipolar or concerned about a family member or friend?

A. Two things: (1) Read the appropriate booklet from the NIMH (see web address above) and (2) Know that you're not alone. Help is available; if you reach out, someone will be there for you. For instance, the National Alliance on Mental Illness has a help line that's staffed Monday through Friday during business hours: 1-800-950-NAMI.

If you're experiencing a major crisis, dial 911 or go to the nearest hospital emergency room.

Q. What should I do if someone mentions they're thinking of suicide?

A. Mention of suicidal thoughts should always be taken seriously. Please refer that person to the National Suicide Prevention Lifeline at 1-800-273-TALK (273-8255).

Q. What percentage of people with untreated bipolar depression die of suicide?

A. About 15 percent, according to Dr. Mark I. Levy of the University of California, San Francisco (UCSF).

Q. Please give a link to a good article about suicide and its prevention.

A. See the resources here, at livescience.com[8]

Q. What is bipolar disorder, in a nutshell?

A. It's a mental disorder that causes a person to bounce erratically between two extreme moods: mania (hopped-up energy to a point where you're losing touch with reality) and depression (a trough of low-energy grayness that can veer into suicidal thoughts).

For a bipolar person, mania is a super-charged "I can do anything" feeling (and/or extreme irritability) that can last for weeks or months. Depression, for a bipolar person, is gray bleakness that can also last for weeks or months.

Here's a definition from a brochure published by the NIMH:

> Bipolar disorder, also known as manic-depressive illness, is a brain disorder that causes unusual shifts in mood, energy, activity levels and the ability to carry out daily tasks. Symptoms of bipolar disorder can be severe. They are different from the normal ups and downs that everyone goes through from time to time. Bipolar disorder symptoms can result in damaged relationships, poor job or school performance, and even suicide.

Q. Is bipolar disorder difficult to diagnose?

A. Yes. Many people endure years of needless suffering before their condition is properly diagnosed and treated. (I'm one of those people.) I believe the medical community has a responsibility to inform itself fully about bipolar illness and the differences between bipolar and other psychological conditions. (Misdiagnosis does happen. According to a major study published in 2014, 12 million American adults are misdiagnosed every year for a variety of physical and psychological conditions. In half of these cases, the misdiagnosis has the potential to result in serious harm. Among the reasons for this shocking number: doctor's visits are too rushed and patients don't provide a full and accurate history.)

Q. Can bipolar disorder be cured?

A. No, not yet. But the symptoms can be managed effectively.

Q. What causes bipolar disorder?

A. A chemical imbalance in the brain. We don't know yet what causes this imbalance. The disorder might be genetically based and environmentally triggered.

Q. Are we any closer to finding the exact cause today than 30 years ago?

A. Yes. There's a lot of research being done, and it's yielding insight, but we've got a long way to go, given that the human brain is the most complex biological system in the universe, and given the fierce competition for resources in health care research. Some scientists estimate that we know only 20 to 30 percent today of all that can be known about the brain.

Q. How common is bipolar disorder?

A. The statistics are complicated, but a reasonable estimate is that 2 to 3 percent of Americans have it — perhaps nine million people. Perhaps one percent of the global population has it.

Q. That number seems too high to me. I don't know anyone who's bipolar.

A. Actually, you probably do. It's not something that's instantly obvious.

Q. Is the disorder growing in prevalence?

A. We're not sure.

Q. Why is the percentage of bipolar people higher in America than worldwide?

A. We're not sure.

Q. Is the rate of bipolar disorder different among genders?

A. No. All genders suffer at about the same rate.

Q. Can bipolar be self-diagnosed, i.e., can I decide for myself if I'm bipolar based on my reading of articles and my answers to online questionnaires?

A. No. You need to get a professional diagnosis and treatment. That said, some online questionnaires are useful as a first step toward seeing a health professional. One such test is available here. [9]

Q. What are some offshoots of bipolar disorder?

A. Substance abuse is a big one, including alcoholism, methamphetamine addiction and opioid addiction, and anxiety disorders as well. People with bipolar disorder, because of the medications they take, are at higher risk for thyroid disease, diabetes, heart disease and other physical illnesses. The suicide rate for bipolar people is also higher than among the general population.

Q. Which is correct, "bipolar disorder" or "bipolar illness"?

A. They're both correct. The condition was known for most of the 20th century as manic depression and is still referred to that way in some books and pamphlets. "Bipolar disorder" became the most accepted term in 1980; it's more precise and carries less emotional baggage than manic depression.

Q. Can you elaborate on the symptoms of bipolar disorder?

A. To quote from the National Institute of Mental Health: "People with bipolar disorder experience unusually intense emotional states that occur in distinct periods called 'mood episodes.' Each mood episode represents a drastic change from a person's usual mood and behavior. An overly joyful or overexcited state is called a manic episode, and an extremely sad or hopeless state is called a depressive episode. Sometimes, a mood episode includes symptoms of both mania and depression. This is called a mixed state. Extreme changes in energy, activity, sleep, and behavior go along with these changes in mood."

Q. Are bipolar people dangerously wacky? Crazy?

A. Bipolar people are no more likely to be dangerously wacky or "crazy" than other population groups. Bipolar does not equate to craziness or homicidal tendencies.

Q. Hey, Vincent van Gogh was pretty darn wacky! He cut off his ear!

A. The medical community in his day, the 1870s and '80s, didn't have any good ways to treat the disease. We have such ways today — pharmacological and psychotherapeutic techniques that are safe and effective and allow people with the illness to live full and productive lives.

Q. If van Gogh had treated his disease, would he still have become van Gogh? Would he have been a great artist? Did the disease somehow help him become great?

A. This is a fascinating question. We really don't know how van Gogh would have responded to the right medications. Perhaps if he had received excellent treatment, he would have created great paintings for three decades rather than three years.

The links between bipolar disorder and creativity are much studied. The writer Shadi-Sade Sarreshtehdarzadeh, who is bipolar, offers a summary: "Recent psychological studies have shown that those with bipolar disorder are disproportionately overrepresented in creative occupations. The exact link between the two is still to be discovered, but there is a belief that those with bipolar have a unique way of perceiving the world that is perhaps more sensitive to certain things and experiences than the average person."

I examine creativity at length in my chapter titled "My Adventures With Creativity." A good book on the link between mental illness and creativity is *The Creating Brain: The Neuroscience of Genius* by Nancy Andreasen (2005).

The larger question here is, are there good things about being bipolar? Many people who suffer from the affliction say there's nothing whatsoever that's good about it; as noted, some people who have this condition, and aren't treated properly, descend into such agony they kill themselves. On the other hand, for some people, the highs of the disorder can be periods of substantial achievement. Sarreshtehdarzadeh summarizes this paradox nicely. She notes the positives — creativity, ambition, energy, productivity and sharp thinking — but adds that the illness is "mostly negative." I agree with that.

Q. Can stress trigger bipolar symptoms?

A. Yes. And, conversely, stress reduction has been found useful by some bipolar folks in reducing symptoms. Exercise is great for stress reduction, along with meditation, plenty of sleep and good nutrition.

Q. You mention meditation several times in this book. Can you talk a bit more about it?

A. I will quote from an article about meditation that appeared on the first page of the "Review" section in the *Wall Street Journal* in July 2017. The article, by Robert Wright, is based on his book *Why Buddhism Is True: The Science and Philosophy of Meditation and Enlightenment* (2017). The article's headline is "The Meditation Cure: A basic practice of Buddhism turns out to be one of the best ways to deal with the anxieties and appetites bequeathed to us by our evolutionary history." The author writes:

> Mindfulness meditation is an exercise in attention. It involves calming the mind — typically by focusing on the breath — and then using the resulting equanimity to observe things with unusual care and clarity. The things observed can include sounds, physical sensations or anything else in the field of awareness. ... Perhaps most important is the careful observation of feelings, because feelings play such a powerful

role in guiding our perceptions, thought and behavior. ... Mindfulness meditation, Buddhists say, can change our perspective on feelings such as anxiety and rage and thereby sap their power to warp our vision and make us suffer. [These claims] are now getting important support from evolutionary psychology, the modern study of how natural selection engineered the human mind. ... Mindfulness calls for a kind of skepticism toward feelings. Rather than automatically following their guidance, you critically examine them and decide which ones to trust. Evolutionary psychology helps to explain why this skepticism is warranted — why so many feelings are unreliable guides.

Wright goes on to explain that natural selection — Darwin's great idea, the process that created us over millions of years of evolution — "is indifferent to whether we are happy or sad, enlightened or deluded." Its sole agenda is getting genes into the next generation. To further that goal in humans, it makes use of feelings — for example, anxiety. Sometimes, anxiety is essential (for instance, a Paleolithic mom worrying that her child may have wandered off into the forest, or a modern-day mom worrying about her child wandering off down the street). But often, anxiety isn't necessary at all. Often we experience an excess of anxiety, a mismatch between what natural selection has given us to get genes into the next generation and what we need in our current environment. The modern environment, says Wright, has a very large capacity to "warp our feelings about, hence our perception of, the world." (Buddhists call this "illusion.") Meditation can straighten out that mismatch, can heal our capacity for illusion, by teaching us to observe our feelings and choose what's appropriate. If we choose to be skeptical of excess anxiety, we can reduce its grip, and thus reduce stress.

Wright's book provides not only deep background on the value of meditation but instruction in how to do it. I recommend it to anyone who needs to reduce stress (i.e., pretty much everybody!).

The David Lynch Foundation[10] is another good resource for people interested in meditation.

Q. Proper breathing is a good way to reduce stress, right?

A. Right. Breathing matters big-time. Here's an interesting quote from Dr. Andrew Weil: "If I had to limit my advice on healthier living to just one tip, it would be simply to learn how to breathe correctly." Weil has created a good CD, *Breathing: The Master Key to Self Healing* (1999). A good book on this topic is *Breathe* by Belisa Vranich (2016).

Q. Can help for bipolar illness be found in alternative approaches?

A. Some people think so. Dr. Joseph Mercola summarizes the alternative perspective on his website[11].

For another web page with information about alternative tactics, go to alternativedepressiontherapy.com[12]

A search for the words "natural" and "bipolar" at Amazon.com will produce a list of books.

Q. Tom Cruise went on "The Today Show" in 2005 and bashed the taking of psychiatric drugs. What's your view of his remarks?

A. I think they're idiotic. Dr. Levy of UCSF called Cruise's comments "tremendously destructive." And I'll quote Dr. Ken Duckworth, medical director for NAMI: "Tom Cruise and I have almost nothing in common on how we see mental health conditions. ... He encourages people to exercise. ... There is some data that shows exercise does help persons with mild to moderate depression. ... Now can aerobic exercise help people with treatment-resistant, severe depression? Never alone. And I mean NEVER alone."

Q. What if my medications don't work?

A. Keep trying with different medications. To again quote Ken Duckworth of NAMI: "Keep on trying new medicines, and you are likely to hit one over time that works. Is it arduous? Of course. Is it unpleasant? You bet. Is it unfortunate that we don't have the kind of genetic mapping that can say how you are going to respond to a certain medication? Yes." Duckworth recommends that people facing this dilemma get an independent consultation with an expert: "Go to the local academic medical center. Go to the depression center. Most academic medical centers do have such capacity." Duckworth also encourages such people to increase their efforts in non-pharmacological areas such as talk therapy and exercise.

Q. Do we know exactly why drugs work, when they work?

A. No, we don't. We don't have the neurology mapped out. People want to know exactly how medications work and get upset when they're told, "Scientists just don't know."

Q. Does a feeling of shame invariably accompany the disorder?

A. Not invariably, but many people who have the condition feel ashamed. Some of this feeling stems from media portrayals of bipolar people, which tend to be negative and simplistic.

Q. Can bipolar illness get worse without good treatment?

A. Yes.

Q. Can you cite additional articles on the Internet that provide accurate information? Also, do you have a book list?

A. Here you go:

- The article "Could It Be Bipolar? Seven Signs to Look For"[13] on healthline.com.

- The article "9 Myths of Bipolar Disorder"[14] on psychcentral.com, which also has a good list of books on bipolar illness.

- The article "Disease or Madness: Society's Perception of Bipolar Disorder"[15] (includes an interesting "Comments" section) on the Serendip Studio website.

- A number of articles[16] on EverydayHealth.com.

- For serious students of bipolar illness, an outstanding college-level textbook is "Manic-Depressive Illness: Bipolar Disorders and Recurrent Depression" by Frederick K. Goodwin and Kay Redfield Jamison (second edition, Oxford University Press, 2007).

1. **Winston Churchill link to an interesting article**
    (www.bipolar-lives.com/winston-churchill-and-manic-depression.html)

2. **Vincent van Gogh was likely bipolar. A paper presented by Dr. Joseph Calabrese**
    (https://vimeo.com/112001360)

3. **View performance of "The Starry Night" by Don McLean and the visual picture "Vincent van Gogh's "Starry Starry Night."**
    (https://www.youtube.com/watch?v=DD1ih3Q9otE)

4. **The Rainforest Action Network fact sheet on palm oil**
    (https://www.ran.org/palm_oil?gclid=EAIaIQobChMIuYr_j67Y1wIVl1YNCh2ktQ_lEAAYASAAEgLgXvD_BwE)

5. **NAMI Homepage** (https://www.nami.org/)

6. **NAMI Cleveland** (https://namigreatercleveland.org/)

7. **One website that offers good information on bipolar disorder**
    (https://www.nimh.nih.gov/health/publications/bipolar-disorder-listing.shtml)

8. **Article about suicide and its prevention**
    (https://www.livescience.com/44615-suicide-help.html)

9. **Can bipolar be self-diagnosed?**
    (www.dbsalliance.org/pdfs/MDQ.pdf)

10. **The David Lynch Foundation: The value of meditation and instructions on how**
    (https://www.davidlynchfoundation.org/)

11. **Dr. Joseph Mercola the alternative approaches to bipolar disorder.**
    (https://articles.mercola.com/sites/articles/archive/2016/06/02/supplements-for-mental-health.aspx)

12. **Alternative Depression Therapy**
    (http://www.alternativedepressiontherapy.com/alternative-bipolar-treatment.html)

13. **"Could It Be Bipolar? Seven Signs to Look For"**
    (https://www.healthline.com/health/could-it-be-bipolar-signs-to-look-for#Overview1)

14. **"9 Myths of Bipolar Disorder"**
    (https://psychcentral.com/blog/archives/2009/06/12/9-myths-of-bipolar-disorder/)

15. **"Disease or Madness: Society's Perception of Bipolar Disorder"**
    (serendip.brynmawr.edu/exchange/aeraeber/disease-or-madness-societys-perception-bipolar-disorder)

16. **A number of articles on bipolar disorder**
    (https://www.everydayhealth.com/bipolar-disorder/articles.aspx)

Made in the USA
Monee, IL
19 September 2022

14276428R00083